# INCREASE YOUR INCOME

## AND WEALTH

## BUYING APARTMENT

## BUILDINGS

# INCREASE

# YOUR INCOME

# AND WEALTH

# BUYING APARTMENT

# BUILDINGS

By

Jeffrey B. Moore

RIVERCROSS PUBLISHING, INC.
Orlando

ISBN: 1-58141-048-4

Library of Congress Catalog Card Number: 00-042506

Third Printing

**Library of Congress Cataloging-in-Publication Data**

Moore, Jeffrey B., 1957-
    Increase your income and wealth buying apartment build-
            ings / Jeffrey B. Moore.
        p. cm.
    ISBN 1-58141-048-4
    1. Apartment houses—United States. 2. Real estate in-
            vestment—United States. I. Title.

HD259 .M66 2000
332.63'24- - dc21

                                        00-042506

Editor: Juliette Moore
Jacket photograph by Ernest C. Withers Photography, Mem-
            phis, Tennessee

# TABLE OF CONTENTS

Acknowledgments        7
Foreword        11
Introduction        15
Chapter 1: A Unique Investment        21
Chapter 2: Is Income Important to You?        28
Chapter 3: A Permanent Income Source for You        35
Chapter 4: Variety is the Spice of Ownership        46
Chapter 5: Where Can I Find These Jewels?        49
Chapter 6: Looking at the Numbers        60
Chapter 7: Let's Make a Deal (It Takes Courage!)        71
Chapter 8: Financing Opportunities - "There's Money
        Everywhere!"        83
Chapter 9: Duplexes - Everybody Should Know        91
Chapter 10: Creative Financing        95
Chapter 11: Tax Deferred Exchanges        101
Chapter 12: May We Close Now?        105
Chapter 13: Managing for Maximum Income        108
Chapter 14: The Missing Ingredient        117
Index        121

# ACKNOWLEDGMENTS

I would like to first acknowledge my heavenly Father, God almighty, for richly blessing me with the family, friends, the intellect, and the athletic gifts that have shaped my life to this day. As I look back over my life, I am truly in awe at the way You have kept me, protected me, and gifted me. You continue to carry me and look past my faults and see my needs. I can never repay You for what you've done for me. You've been LORD, you've been so faithful!

My family, I thank you all from the depths of my heart.

Chief, thank you for exposing me to real estate and thank you for your love, encouragement, and support. Essie, thank you for the motherly advice and wisdom you have so lovingly shared over the years.

Joan, thank you for showing me how to love family and friends, and how to give of myself without expectation of reward other than the satisfaction of knowing I was helpful. Thanks for that beautiful smile.

My bride Juliette, you have shown me through our relationship, that love can be truly awesome and beautiful and not just fantasy on the movie screen or in a non-fiction novel. I thank you for your friendship, kindness, and your inspiring support. It has been an awesome journey watching you take OASIS to new heights. You are the wind beneath my wings! I love you deeply!

Steve, thanks for showing me how to verbalize my love. It's one thing to feel it, and it's another thing to have the courage to say it. You were the best tackle the New England Patriots ever had.

Regina, thank you for your example of unselfishness, thoughtfulness for your siblings, and kindness. Thank you for setting the example for academic excellence and achievement. Thank you for *always* being there when I need you.

Terry, thank you for your love and support. You've always been there to listen to my challenges. You've shown me what it means to be a friend and loyal family member.

Vince, thank you for your love and support. It has been a joy watching you grow from a little boy whose diapers I changed to a fine young man. I admire your discipline and courage. Thanks for helping to establish the wide receiver legacy at the University of Tennessee. Kendrick, my *main man*, I am so proud of the young man that you have become. I appreciate your strength and I'm so grateful that you realize that it's okay to be a genius. I am excited about your future. Keep up the good work!

Stefanie (my sweet angel), I thank you for your love and understanding. Your gift of poetic expression has been an inspiration to me and you continue to amaze me with your level of maturity. Your future accomplishments are truly unlimited.

Toya, it has been a joy watching you recognize your intellectual and athletic gifts. You are a beautiful young lady with awesome talent and a magnetic personality. Continue to strive for excellence–you have what it takes.

Keith, my little partner, you have the gift of a kind heart and an excellent mind. There is no limit to what you can do with those unique gifts. Remember, there are *no* shortcuts to greatness.

To Stella, thank you for picking up where Joan asked you to in giving the support and love that I've needed. I appreciate you always being there.

To the rest of my family and friends, Chuck, Jock, Teddy, Alex, Paul, Reggie, Ebone, Jordan, and Anthony, I love you all.

To Ron and Pat, you have been excellent mentors and a great source of wisdom and support for me. May you continue to enjoy prosperity and God's divine favor.

To Alvin, you have been a true friend to me and you continue to inspire me to reach higher and higher. May God continue to shower his blessings on you, Carla, Heather, and Phillip.

To my real estate investment partners, Mike Fearnley, Cary Califf, and Dan Henley, thank you for your confidence in me. I am enjoying this journey that we're on and excited about the possibilities for the future.

To my original Master Mind Partners, Herman, Glenn, Derek, A.J., Lonnie, Sye, Alvin, Dan, and Trent, thanks for your encouragement love and support.

To my football and basketball coaches, Bob Hewitt, Red Ross, J. B. Payton, Tim Morgan, Art

Kuntzman, Bill Battle, Bob Harrison, Johnny Majors, and Lionel Taylor, thank you for challenging me, pushing me, and teaching me the lessons of preparation and hard work.

To my real estate mentors, Bob Walz, Rich Heine, Jan Withee, Roy Adams, Harold Crye, Dick Leike, William Mitchell, Dan Whipple, Charlie Callis, Chet Whitsitt, and Judy McLellan, thank you all for the opportunity to work with some of the finest individuals in the real estate industry. You have inspired me to be the best I can be.

# Foreword

Jeff is a man who is committed, dedicated and true to his word. He is also one who enjoys life, loving his family and selling apartment buildings. His character is not defined without mentioning real estate investment. His passion for real estate is inevitably the driving force of his accomplishments. His strong will to succeed has propelled me to become the best business partner that I can be. He is a powerful, confident, polished man, and many consider him to be a major contribution to their success in real estate investment. He has set the example that athletes do not have to become average after they make their final jump shot on the basketball court or score their last touchdown on the football field. Being a wide receiver with the Los Angeles Rams has instilled in my husband the diligence needed for prosperity. The experience of playing in the National Football League has challenged Jeff to become better than average. It has summoned him to take the real estate career and make it a rewarding and exciting adventure.

As I meditate on the word "wealth," I reflect on an abundance of valuable substances: having more than enough. Wealth is any commodity that has a value that you can exchange for something else of value. Becoming wealthy is a deep desire for many of us; we hope it will happen—one day! In this book, Jeff tells how one can increase his or her income at any age—young or old. Making your dreams come true is not something you need to put off until a later time in life. The key is to start mapping your successes while you are still in the dream stage. Begin right now to make a firm decision to produce progress every day. Eventually, you'll see that you've accomplished tremendous results.

When Jeff and I began our career purchasing apartment buildings, we started by investing in duplexes and four-plexes. It was quite easy managing the buildings, so we decided to invest in larger buildings—up to 32 units. In order to stay focused and maintain our discipline, it became necessary to write down our goals. In the course of defining our prospects, we shared the excitement of investing in more apartment communities. Investing in apartment buildings can be a second career, begun even while your primary career is still being established.

I challenge more women to consider duplexes and apartment buildings as a valid investment for your future and one you can leave to your children. I believe that women have a gift given by the Creator to take care of the needs of others. This is one of the best opportunities to be nurturers and reap rewarding benefits at the same time. We have the natural talents to decorate and enhance our homes, our gardens, our businesses, even ourselves, with very meager resources. We are able to maintain what we have and cultivate it into something greater. This same aptitude can contribute to the beautification of your apartment buildings.

Owning apartment buildings with your mate is a wonderful business opportunity where two people can come together and contribute equally to making decisions that will enhance the quality of their union.

I know that the enterprise you decide to build together can be an exciting and remarkable journey. I wish you much success with your apartment buildings!

Juliette Moore

# INCREASE
# YOUR INCOME
# AND WEALTH
# BUYING APARTMENT
# BUILDINGS

# INTRODUCTION

My father has been in the real estate business in Memphis, Tennessee, for over 30 years. He has sold houses, built houses, managed them as rental properties, and rehabbed them for resale. He still continues to be actively involved in the real estate business to this day.

As a result, I grew up being exposed to the real estate business and believing that one day I would go in to the business selling houses as my father had always done.

Ironically, through the grace of God, my athletic career took me on a unique path, and my sports career and real estate career collided. The collision resulted in my specialization in a fascinating area of real estate investment.

Let me explain. In high school, I was blessed with the talent and teammates to become Athlete of the Year in my hometown of Memphis. As a result, I was heavily recruited by many of the major colleges in the

15

South and offered scholarships to play football at those colleges.

My mother, Erma Joan Moore, now deceased, taught school in Memphis for over 25 years and always emphasized to me and my siblings the importance of education and making good grades. Therefore, I was a pretty good student in school. In fact, all of her children went to major universities, and all but one, graduated with at least a bachelor's degree. My oldest sister, Monice, went on to obtain a law degree and now closes most of our real estate transactions at one of the most successful law firms here in Memphis, Fearnley & Califf, PLLC.

After high school, I chose the University of Tennessee because of their great football tradition. During my first two years of college, I simply did enough to get by. My focus was more on football than on my grades. However, just prior to my junior year, I woke up and realized that the chances of my becoming a professional football player, which was a long time dream of mine, were not that great. This awakening made me realize that I had better get serious about my school work and focus on a career after sports. That's when I started paying serious attention to my academics. It was during this time that I started to think about my major course of study in school. I decided to major in Real Estate and Urban Development. I then had to take courses in that field, and one of the courses I took introduced me to the world of commercial real estate. Until that time, I was totally unaware that this area of opportunity existed. I became exposed to the concept or notion of selling multi-million dollar investment properties vs. single family homes. This was very interesting and exciting to me.

During the time that I started to get serious about my school work, my athletic career started to take off. I had a great junior and senior year as a starting wide receiver at the University of Tennessee, a.k.a. "Wide Receiver University." Before long, sports agents were contacting me telling me that I was one of the highest rated wide receivers in the country, and I would be drafted into the NFL. This was a dream come true for me. Several teams flew coaches into Knoxville to have me work out for them. I also had to fly to New York and Chicago to take a physical for the NFL teams.

It was during a flight to New York that I first received a revelation into what my future career after sports would be. I was seated next to a well-dressed gentleman on the flight, and we started to chat. In our conversation, we talked about football and why I was going to New York. We also talked about real estate and what I would do after my career was over. He made a profound statement to me during our conversation. He told me that I could sell real estate just about anywhere in the country; however, he said if I wanted to learn to be one of the "best at commercial real estate," I needed to go to either New York or Los Angeles. That statement stuck with me because at the time, no one from either of the California teams or the New York teams had contacted me and expressed an interest in my playing for them. Ironically, I was drafted into the NFL by the Los Angeles Rams. This was less than a month after the stranger I had met on the plane had made that profound statement to me regarding learning to be one of the "best in commercial real estate."

I moved to California during the summer of 1979 and started my professional career as a wide receiver with the Los Angeles Rams. The following year, I started my career as a commercial real estate agent during the off-season from football, working in the commercial division of a large residential real estate firm.

That year, I closed my first real estate transaction as an agent on a 4-unit apartment building. I was hooked on apartment buildings from that time on. I went on to specialize in the sale of apartment buildings. I noticed early on that the most successful agents in the business were those who focused on one particular aspect of real estate and specialized in that area. Therefore, rather than trying to sell land, office buildings, shopping centers, or anything that came across my desk, I focused on apartment buildings.

I later joined New Dimension Properties where I met one of my mentors in this uniquely specialized area of commercial real estate. Bob Walz is the founder of New Dimension Properties in Southern California, a real estate office that specializes in the sale and exchange of apartment buildings. It was under Bob's tutelage that my commercial real estate career took off.

After 13 years in Southern California, developing skills as a specialist in the sale of apartment buildings, I returned to my hometown of Memphis to rejoin my family and to apply what I had learned to the marketplace in Memphis.

I discovered that Memphis was a gold mine of opportunities for investors interested in apartment buildings. Since 1992, I have worked in Memphis specializing in the sale of apartment buildings and duplexes.

Therefore, it is with the experience of closing over $100 million in real estate transactions involving apartment buildings and duplexes that I share this book with you.

One of my main objectives in writing this work is to inform, encourage, and enlighten readers on the benefits of increasing one's income and wealth through the ownership of apartment buildings.

I believe that anyone who is seriously interested in the area of investment in apartment buildings and duplexes will benefit from reading this book.

It comes from a unique perspective because of the markets I have been privileged to work in. Memphis and the Orange County market in Southern California, are uniquely different markets.

The book possesses a different flavor also due to my background in sports, as well as the fact that there are not many individuals in this country, particularly African-American, who have chosen to specialize in this area of commercial real estate.

Throughout the book I have provided pictures and a brief profile of actual transactions that have occurred in recent years. Their purpose is to give you an idea of the diversity of transactions that take place in this industry on a regular basis. I hope that they will serve to inspire and enlighten you.

I thank you for choosing this work to include in your library of knowledge and hope that you benefit richly from the information provided herein.

# CHAPTER 1 - A UNIQUE INVESTMENT

Real Estate has long been considered one of the safest long-term investments that an individual can make. However, the term "real estate" can cover so many areas and property types. Single family homes, office buildings, shopping centers, land, industrial buildings, warehouses, churches, retail stores, and of course, my favorite, apartment buildings, are all considered real estate.

For the purposes of this book, we are going to focus on what has been proven to be one of the most profitable and accessible forms of real estate available in America today for investment and income purposes. In fact, outside of the single family house and land, there are more apartment buildings in the United States than any other type of real estate. To take it even a step further, for investment purposes, there seems to be more money invested in apartment buildings in this country than in any other type of real estate.

Apartment buildings provide an opportunity for individuals like you and me to gain access to real estate investment ownership. There is more diversity in apartment buildings by far than there are in the other real estate types. An individual can own anywhere from a duplex consisting of two apartments, up to a complex containing several hundred apartments, depending on their individual financial capabilities. There is plenty of money available for financing apartment buildings. Most lenders will lend an individual money on a higher loan-to-value basis for apartment buildings than for most other real estate, which makes the down payment requirements much less.

16 Units – Colorado - Memphis, Tennessee
Recent Purchase Price:    $80,000
Closing Date: August, 1997
Unit Mix    16-1 bedroom 1 bath
Scheduled Monthly Rents    $2,400

Why are apartment buildings much more popular with investors and lenders? The answer to that question speaks to the unique character of apartment buildings. You see, apartment buildings are *commercial* in that they

22

are a business that generates revenue to the owner in the form of rents. They are also residential in that individuals occupy these properties as a form of *shelter*, which is one of the basic human needs. This residential aspect of apartment buildings thus contributes to the high demand for the use of this property type by a very large market. Therefore, you have a property that is in high demand for its use that generates income to the owner. This explains why the occupancy rate is typically higher and the risk of ownership is reduced.

As I mentioned before, there are a variety of apartment buildings available to the individual investor. This is a very significant point because all other forms of real estate investment do not have nearly the diversity of apartment buildings. In my career, I have sold income

4 Units - 22nd Street - Huntington Beach, California
Recent Purchase Price:　　　$572,825
Closing Date: July, 1999
Unit Mix　　　3-2 bedroom 1.5 bath
　　　　　　　1-3 bedroom 2.5 bath
Scheduled Monthly Rents　　$3,300

properties from duplexes up to apartment buildings of 60 units or more. I have also had the good fortune of selling buildings that consisted of over 100 units. The point is that there is an apartment building out there that fits most financial situations. One merely has to determine what they have available to invest and get busy looking at the properties that fit that criterion. You may decide that you want to get a partner so that you can acquire a bigger property than you otherwise would. Having a partner could also enable you to share the risk and responsibility of your first building with someone else.

Depending on the type of building you plan to start with, you could have some rather attractive financing options available to you. For example, most lenders are willing to loan up to 90% of the price on a two to four-unit building if one of the units will be occupied by the owner. In the Memphis market, we also have lenders that will loan up to 90% on 2-4 units, even if the owner does not occupy one of the units. This financing has contributed to a large increase in the sale of duplexes and 4-plexes in our market.

I have found that most individual investors tend to prefer 2 to 4-unit apartment buildings, primarily because they are easier to finance, and they tend to be a good way to start gaining experience in operating an apartment building. Management is usually not as much of a challenge when you have 2 to 4 tenants to satisfy vs. 20 or more. An investor can usually get started with less cash outlay with 2 to 4-unit buildings.

Of course, a lot depends on the market you happen to live in or plan to invest in. My experience in apartment buildings comes from having worked in two very different markets. In the Southern California market, I completed deals in Orange County, Riverside County, and San Bernardino County. I am currently actively completing transactions in Memphis, Tennessee, in the Shelby County area. These areas represent a major contrast in price ranges. I have sold duplexes in Shelby County for as little as $15,000 and duplexes in the California market for $300,000. It was all relative to an extent though, because where the $300,000 duplex could demand rents of $1,600 per apartment or more, the $15,000 duplex might rent for $250 or more. Sometimes that type of range in price could occur in the same market. For example, in the Memphis market, one can buy a duplex for $15,000, or pay as much as $250,000. In Southern California, a duplex can sell for as little as

6 Units – Evergreen - Memphis, Tennessee
Recent Purchase Price:      $60,000
Closing Date: April, 1999
Unit Mix      6-2 bedroom 1 bath
Scheduled Monthly Rents     $1,200

$75,000, or as much as $500,000 for a duplex in one of the Beach cities.

What has been interesting to me is that I've met individuals throughout my career who have been successful in operating their buildings in all segments of the market. They find a niche that they are comfortable with and they continue to acquire properties that fit their niche.

I have also been fascinated by meeting and working with individuals who specialize in owning and operating duplexes. Then I've worked with individuals who prefer the bigger buildings.

Regardless of whether it was larger buildings or smaller buildings, I've always found it interesting to meet owners who seem to enjoy their business and seem to do a good job at it. One thing these individuals have in common is that once they determined the kind of building they liked, they continued to acquire and operate that same building type.

We have owned and operated several different building types—duplexes, 4-plexes, a 15-unit, a 16-unit, a 26-unit, a 29-unit, a 73-unit, a 92-unit, and a 123-unit building. Each building has its own characteristics. Some buildings have all 1-bedroom apartments and some have all 2-bedroom units. Some of those buildings have central air and heat. Some have wall heaters and window air conditioners. In some buildings we provide appliances, and in some buildings, the residents provide all of the appliances. I share this information to emphasize that there is no one apartment building type that is uniquely more advantageous than the other. You just have to determine what meets your needs and lifestyle best.

The market is wide open. Once you get started, you can determine what works best for you and enjoy the benefits that so many thousands of investors enjoy every day through the successful ownership and management of apartment buildings throughout this country.

28 Units - Acacia Avenue - Fontana, California
Recent Purchase Price:       $935,000
Closing Date: June, 1999
Unit Mix       All-2 bedroom 1 bath
Monthly Rental Income       $15,400

# CHAPTER 2 - IS INCOME IMPORTANT TO YOU?

You need to have $360,000 in cash to produce an income of $1,500 per month at 5% interest. Will you save that amount over your working career? This chapter may well be the most important chapter in the book. That's because I believe that many Americans tend to be unaware of the significant and fundamental difference between having *cash* and having alternative sources of income. Cash, defined here, means a lump sum of money, vs. income, meaning a steady source of payments to us from some particular source or from various sources.

I think most people would agree that for the average working individual in America, the major portion of their income comes from one source. That source is usually their job. Statistics suggest that for most people, the income from their job barely meets their expenses. There is usually very little remaining for savings, investments, etc. It has been documented that Americans have a very low savings rate compared to most other industrialized countries.

Let's take these two facts of life together: 1) The fact that we have one source of income--usually our jobs, and 2) the fact that we save very little. This suggests that for most of us, we are *very dependent* on that job for our survival and livelihood. It's no surprise that a great deal of stress would occur if that *one source* of income was taken away or disrupted for an extended period of time.

In your own personal situation, how long would you survive under those circumstances given your financial picture? I'm sure it's a very disturbing thought to ponder for most people. The fact of the matter is that we

29 Units - Wellington Avenue - Memphis, Tennessee
Recent Purchase Price:       $340,000
Closing Date: July, 1999
Unit Mix       1-1 bedroom 1 bath
28-2 bedroom 1 bath
Scheduled Monthly Rents    $7,250

are *dependent* on our jobs for our survival in America today. Without our jobs, most of us would not have the resources to provide ourselves and our families with the basic necessities of life: food, clothing, and shelter.

Let's also consider that if this is true for most of us, we are in this endless loop of having income meet our expenses with very little savings or investment. For too many people, this pattern continues until they reach retirement age, and then they are dependent on the government, inadequate retirement income from their jobs, or family members to support them in their retirement years. Much too often, this process has repeated itself. Some people have been fortunate enough, however, to have jobs that paid them a retirement income that was sufficient, along with help from Social Security, to allow them to have a fairly comfortable retirement income. This certainly does not represent the majority of Americans, however, according to statistics.

We're living in a new millennium and the most constant thing in the corporate world today is change. We are in an environment of constant change due to downsizing, mergers, and acquisitions, and the stress-related health issues that go along with trying to survive in that type of working environment. I'm sure you know folks who have worked on a job a good portion of their adult lives, only to find out one day that they were either fired or laid off, or in some cases, forced into an early retirement because of a buyout or a change in corporate strategy.

I think that one can easily conclude that to be totally dependent on one job as our *sole source of income* in today's work environment a very risky proposition.

Even if we manage to stay positive, enthusiastic, and focused so that we survive a chaotic work environment, we still have the savings issue to deal with. If you are like most people in this country, you have managed

96 Units - Foothill Boulevard - Fontana, California
Recent Purchase Price:        $4,500,000
Closing Date: August, 1999
Unit Mix        All-2 bedroom 1 bath
and 2 bedroom 2 bath
Scheduled Monthly Income $61,955

to save very little of your income. It's a fact of life that too many of us *spend* much more than we *earn* every year. Have you ever stopped to think how much money you've earned since you started your first job? Consider how much of that you have left. Let's look at the chart below. This assumes a person at age 35 has been working since age 22, and had an increase in income of 5% per year.

31

| Age | Salary |
|-----|--------|
| 22 | $17,000 |
| 23 | 17,850 |
| 24 | 18,742 |
| 25 | 19,679 |
| 26 | 20,663 |
| 27 | 21,697 |
| 28 | 22,782 |
| 29 | 23,921 |
| 30 | 25,117 |
| 31 | 26,373 |
| 32 | 27,692 |
| 33 | 29,076 |
| 34 | 30,530 |
| 35 | <u>32,057</u> |

Total Income      $333,179
Earned of

As you can see, after 14 years in the workforce, that person has earned over $330,000. If our fictitious person is like most people, he has saved less than $16,659 (5% of that income).

The critical point here is that this is the situation for many people in this country. As this pattern continues through the next 25 years, an individual will have earned over $1,000,000 but will have very little to show for it.

Even if the person in the illustration was a disciplined saver, he would have had to save a substantial amount of his cash to be able to replace his income after retirement. Consider the following chart:

| Monthly Income | Savings Rate | Cash Required |
|---|---|---|
| $1,500 | 5% | $360,000 |
| 2,000 | 5% | 480,000 |
| 2,500 | 5% | 600,000 |
| 3,000 | 5% | 720,000 |
| 3,500 | 5% | 840,000 |

The chart assumes a 5% rate, which is somewhat middle of the road, depending on whether the cash is in a money market or mutual fund. Since this assumes you are retired, the money would be in a fairly conservative investment with minimum risk.

I'm sure most people have not considered these numbers. Imagine if you're earning $30,000 a year and would like to maintain a similar income from savings upon retirement. You would need to have $600,000 in cash, earning 5% per year to accomplish that.

The fact of the matter is that it is highly unlikely that we will save enough money in our lifetime to *independently* fund a comfortable retirement. Given the current work and political environment, we are literally rolling the dice if we are depending on our jobs and Social Security to fund our retirement. Income is the main reason that individuals acquire apartment buildings. Many have found that ownership of these properties creates the cash flow needed to supplement the income from a job, thus creating some financial independence.

4 Units - Dorsey Avenue - Fontana, California
Recent Purchase Price:      $185,000
Closing Date: January, 1999
Unit Mix      All-2 bedroom 1 bath

# CHAPTER 3 - A PERMANENT INCOME SOURCE FOR YOU

Imagine yourself reaching retirement or deciding you no longer want to work full time, and instead of your only source of income being your job, you have multiple sources of income. In other words, each month, you would receive a payment from several different individuals. You would truly be independent of your job as the sole source of income. Even if you worked for your employer and you have built up a comfortable retirement income, that's all well and good. The difference here is that your retirement income would be not your sole source of survival. Imagine the peace of mind you would have. Wouldn't it be great? Suppose you could have multiple sources of income ten years before you decided to retire from your job? You still are working every day, but because of a *change in strategy* that you've made, you now have several independent sources of income in addition to your earnings from your employer.

This is the opportunity that is available to you when you own apartment buildings and duplexes. I know that sounds simplistic and, believe me, one of the goals of this book is simplicity. However, I have witnessed this situation for many individuals like yourself who desire to become independent of a single source of income. In my career, since I sold my first property as an agent (which happened to be a 4-unit apartment building in Upland, California), I have closed over $100 million in apartment transactions. The majority of those deals were closed by individuals like yourself who go to work every day on a job of some sort. These individuals had adopted a strategy of creating multiple sources of income through the ownership and control of apartment buildings and duplexes. You can do the same, too.

27 Units – Titus - Memphis, Tennessee
Recent Purchase Price: $500,000
Closing Date: January, 1999
Unit Mix        27-2 bedroom 1 bath
Scheduled Monthly Rents    $9,970

I have clients who own anywhere from a single duplex to some who own over 400 apartment units, and those units represent multiple sources of income they receive every month.

The one thing we all have in common, however, is that we are *totally independent* of a single source of income, whether that source is a job, a business, or a sales career. We all have a strategy that is very simple and that has proven results in helping an individual to increase their income and build wealth. The strategy is simply this:

1. Acquire a *multi-family property (apartment building or duplex)*.

2. Learn to manage the property efficiently, or hire management to ensure you receive the maximum rental income.

3. Use the rental *income to maintain the property* and *pay off the mortgage.*

4. Repeat the process.

Remember the previous chart that describes the amount of cash required for you to replace your present income? With apartment buildings and duplexes, you won't need anywhere near that amount of cash, yet these properties have the ability to provide retirement income well in excess of what you previously determined you would need.

Imagine being on your job ten years from now and having 12 additional sources of income that pay you in excess of what your job pays you. Do you think you would feel differently about your job? Would you feel differently about your life overall? I believe that for most people, our entire outlook on life would change if we were independent of our jobs as a sole source of income. It doesn't necessarily mean that we would not work. Many of us are very dedicated and hard workers who enjoy what we do for a living. However, I believe that a lot of the everyday stress would be relieved and we would start to get more of the juice out of life that's available to us. I know that feeling and there are thousands of individuals who know and enjoy that feeling. My hope is that you will use the information presented here to get to know that feeling for yourself.

34 Units - Date Street - Fontana, California
Recent Purchase Price:      $1,130,000
Closing Date: May, 1999
Unit Mix:      4-1 bedroom 1 bath
30-2 bedroom 1.5 bath
Scheduled Monthly Rental Income  $19,090

4 Units – Aubra - Memphis, Tennessee
Recent Purchase Price:      $37,000
Closing Date: February, 1999
Unit Mix      4-2 bedroom 1 bath
Scheduled Monthly Rents    $940

The strategy is very simple. The more you put it to work, the more independent you will become of that job or business, and the sooner you will start to enjoy the benefits of financial freedom. This is income that will come to you for the rest of your life, or for as long as you continue to own and operate the properties. The critical part of this strategy is that you put it to work for you *while you're working or running a business*. The reason for this is that you want the plan to be in force when you don't need the income from the properties to live on. Your job or business will provide that for you. Your property is then left to generate the income for its own maintenance and, most importantly, for the payoff of the mortgage.

Suppose you borrowed $75,000 from someone and agreed to pay it back over a 15-year period. You took the $75,000 and invested it on the stock market or you spent it on some toy or asset you've been wanting to buy. Now, the next month rolls around and it's time to start repaying the $75,000. However, instead of your paying back the money, a group of your friends get together and agree that they would pay it back for you each month until it was paid in full. Would that be a great deal or what? I'm sure it sounds totally unrealistic in today's society to have friends that generous. Believe it or not, it happens all the time. You see, with the acquisition of an apartment building, an investor borrows the money to buy the property. The residents or tenants, through their rental payments to the investor, pay the money back to the source that it was borrowed from. The idea sounds absurd, but would you believe that it gets even better? The residents in the apartment buildings are more generous than the friends in my earlier example, because they not only pay back the source the money was borrowed from, but they continue to pay even after the loan has been repaid in full. In fact, they continue to pay the investor for as long as he or she owns the building. You can't get more friendly than that. Let me repeat that:

1. Investor finds an apartment building he or she wants to own.
2. Investor finds someone to lend the money to buy the property (up to 90% of the sales price in some cases).
3. Friends (the residents in the building) agree to pay the money back that the investor borrowed.
4. Those friends continue to pay for as long as the investor owns the building.

I'm sure you're wondering where one can find friends so generous that they are willing to do what I described. The fact of the matter is that they are very easy to find. That's because they already live in the building the investor wants to buy before he acquired it. The reason the tenants are so nice is because the investor provides them with a comfortable, respectable place to live. They pay for the privilege of living there. They will continue to pay you or whoever has the determination and drive to want to own that apartment building.

In summary, I'd like to remind you of the strategy I've adopted and strongly recommend to increase your income and build wealth:

11 Units - Richland Street - Upland, California
Recent Purchase Price:      $380,000
Closing Date: May, 1999
Unit Mix      4-1 bedroom 1 bath
7-2 bedroom 2 bath
Scheduled Monthly Rental Income $6,068

1. **Acquire** a multi-family property (apartment building or duplex).
2. **Manage** the property efficiently to insure that you receive the maximum rental income.
3. **Use the rental income** to maintain the property, pay off the mortgage and *own the property free and clear.*
4. **Repeat the process** (as soon as your finances allow you to).

I will talk about management strategies later in the book; however, I want to emphasize one aspect of my strategy that is very critical, and that is the payoff of the mortgage on your apartment building. It's important that you realize that in most markets around the country, the apartment properties you can acquire have cash flow after all expenses, especially if you are putting at

41

least 15-20% down. Do you realize that if you use that cash flow to accelerate the payoff of your mortgage, you speed up the process of becoming independently wealthy?

My personal objective is to pay off the mortgages on my properties over the next ten years. In other words, for each property I acquire, instead of a 15-year, 20-year or 30-year mortgage, my goal is to pay the mortgage off over ten years. Now most people would probably think as I used to think: that if my mortgage payment is based on 20 years, and I decide to pay it off over ten years, I simply double the payment. It makes logical sense, however the numbers don't work that way. Let me illustrate. I buy a 4-unit building for $120,000 and pay $20,000 cash down. My mortgage balance is $100,000. I have the following options to pay off that mortgage:

30-year mortgage @ 8.5% = $ 769 per month

20-year mortgage @ 8.5% = $ 868 per month (13% higher)

10-year mortgage @ 8.5% = $1,240 per month (62% higher)

As you can see, to cut the timeframe to owning the property free and clear by 1/3 from 30 years to 20 years, I simply increase my mortgage payment by 13%. If I want to cut it by 2/3 from 30 years to 10 years, I increase my payment 62% from $769 to $1,240 per month. If my building rents for $450 per month per unit, then my total rent each month would be $1,800. If that is applied to a 10-year mortgage payment strategy, it still leaves $560 per month to cover my other expenses, and if $560 doesn't quite cover it, I use income from other sources to supplement. In summary, over a 10-year period, I'll raise rents enough to cover

Duplex – Kearney - Memphis, Tennessee
Recent Purchase Price:      $44,500
Closing Date: March, 1999
Unit Mix      2-1 bedroom 1 bath
Scheduled Monthly Rent      $610

all the expenses of operating the building. It may be worth it to you to do that knowing that in ten years, you'll no longer have that $1,240 per month payment and you can use that income as you choose to. Owning free and clear multi-family units or apartments is the ultimate in increasing your income and developing wealth.

This mortgage illustration shows how you can use the income from the property to accelerate your wealth by paying off the mortgage much faster than has been done traditionally. Most mortgage loans do not have a pre-pay penalty and this allows you to make additional principal payments. It was quite a surprise to me to realize that by paying an additional 15% above the mortgage payment towards the principal, the loan payoff could be reduced by 1/3 on a 30-year mortgage. Those additional principal payments do not have to be paid monthly, but can be paid any time during the year.

Another variation of this strategy that I've seen put in place is for the owner of an apartment building to use the excess cash flow to accelerate the payoff of the mortgage on his or her personal residence. In this strategy, the investor has determined that the main objective of income property ownership was to eliminate the mortgage payment on his own home as soon as possible.

There are a number of strategies that may be adopted to eliminate mortgage debt on your apartment buildings or other properties. They require excess cash flow that can be generated by your apartment buildings.

In addition to creating a substantial additional source of income, by paying the mortgage over a 10-year period using the income from the property, I have also increased my net worth by a minimum of $120,000. If I have increased the rents over time, the value has also increased. Therefore, a property that I paid $20,000 to acquire is worth at least $120,000 with no debt. That means my investment of $20,000 has increased an average of fifty percent (50%) per year, or $10,000.00 per year. That's an incredible return! So you can see how and why apartment buildings are the most desired commercial real estate in this country. The good news is that you do not have to wait until you have saved a huge amount of cash to get started.

Duplex – Safari - Memphis, Tennessee
Recent Purchase Price:　　$60,000
Closing Date: June, 1999
Unit Mix:　1-2 bedroom 1 bath, 1-3 bedroom 1 bath
Scheduled Monthly Rents　$925

8 Units - Redding Way - Upland, California
Recent Purchase Price:　　$447,500
Closing Date: July, 1999
Unit Mix　　All-2 bedroom 2-bath
Scheduled Monthly Rental Income　$5,210

# CHAPTER 4 - VARIETY IS THE SPICE OF OWNERSHIP

The one thing that sets apartment buildings apart from any other type of investment real estate is the variety of properties available to the marketplace. No other type of commercial real estate can come close to offering this type of variety and versatility. An individual may acquire an apartment building with $5,000 cash to invest or $5,000,000. That is a huge range, and yet it is a fact that the market is broad.

The other aspect of variety involves not only the number of units, but the style and location of the property and how they impact the whole equation. I believe, however, that variety is a good thing. In fact, it's one of the things I enjoy about the business of selling apartment properties. I get the opportunity to work with individuals who are just getting started in the investment area, as well as those who have been at it for a little while and are still building, and with savvy pros who have done lots of transactions over the years and own a substantial portfolio. I also get the privilege or opportunity to see many different types of multi-family properties, and I enjoy looking at apartment buildings. In a way, they are like art. No two buildings are exactly the same. Enough about me and my quirks. The logical question I'm sure that is lurking in your mind with all this variety is, of course, Where do I start? I'm happy to say that I have been asked that question many times over the years and I believe that I have developed the perfect answer to that question. The fact of the matter is that there is no correct answer to the right size and type of property that will work for you. Therefore, the perfect answer is, "I don't know!" However, the advice I always give an individual starting out is to look at as many multi-family properties as you can stand to look at once you determine your price range. Study the building styles, the unit mix (1, 2, or 3 bedroom), the rents, the neighborhood, and the prices. After you've looked at twelve to fifteen properties, you will begin to find some properties with which you feel comfortable.

You can determine your price range by *realistically* looking at the amount of cash you have to work with. Most properties of 2 to 4 units can be bought with a minimum down payment of 10% of the purchase price if the Buyer is obtaining new financing. For example, if you have $10,000 to work with, you can acquire property with up to a $100,000 purchase price. If you have $15,000 down, the price up to 4 units would be $150,000, and so forth.

After a while, you will start to be able to understand rental rates in an area and you can quickly identify a property that has the opportunity to increase in value simply by raising rents to market levels.

Also, I have found that there are some great opportunities in the lower income areas of town. The cost per unit tends to be less. The cash flow is usually strong and you can typically acquire more units and more income for the money. Those properties tend to do well if they are managed efficiently and maintained well. I have clients who have built up substantial incomes for themselves buying these types of buildings. On the other hand, I have some clients who prefer the upscale properties that are in the most expensive areas of town. These owners try to attract a more professional clientele that is willing to pay the highest rental rates in town for a nice and well-maintained apartment in a more exclusive area.

Take the time to educate yourself and you'll reach a comfort level that will allow you to move a step closer to becoming a landlord.

24 Units – Melrose - Memphis, Tennessee
Recent Purchase Price:          $401,500
Closing Date: March, 1999
Unit Mix        24-1 bedroom 1 bath
Scheduled Monthly Rents     $6,405

# CHAPTER 5 - WHERE CAN I FIND THESE JEWELS?

Apartment buildings and duplexes are usually located all over your town. Since you weren't conscious of them, or maybe never considered owning them, you probably drove by them every day and never thought twice about it.

However, now that you have an interest in them, you will undoubtedly start to notice them all over the place. There are a few sources that I would suggest to be the best places to go to find these jewels of economic opportunity. They are: 1) the real estate brokerage community, 2) the classified ads, and 3) networking.

The real estate brokerage community in most parts of the country is going to be your best source of opportunities. In most markets, individuals can engage an agent or broker to find the multi-family properties or duplexes that are available in their particular area. Usually, that agent can not only find the properties that are available on the market, but also the properties that sold, prices they sold for, and rents at the time the properties sold, etc. This is valuable information in getting one educated as to what the market is about. It helps to know the market from a sales standpoint, as well as what rental rates are in the areas you are considering.

In most of the larger markets around the country near major cities, there are usually a few individual brokers or agents who specialize in the sale of multi-family properties. If you can locate one of these individuals, they usually can give some good insight on what is happening in your particular marketplace. These individuals can usually be found by asking around the real estate agent community.

14 Units - Alpine Street - Upland, California
Recent Purchase Price:          $587,000
Closing Date: July, 1999
Unit Mix: 7-1 bedroom 1 bath
7-2 bedroom 2 bath
Scheduled Monthly Rental Income  $7,375

They usually advertise in your local newspaper. Their ads are usually found in the "investment property for sale" or "income property for sale" sections of the classified ads in your local paper. Call these individuals and talk with them about the opportunities available in your area. Some of the questions you would want to ask are as follows:

50

1.     Where can I find duplexes and apartment buildings in the area in a certain price range? (determined by the amount of cash you have available)

2.     What are the prices of those properties?

3.     What are the rents in those properties?

4.     Who are the best lenders to work with for this type of property?

This is a brief list of questions, however, this is all you need to know until you get out and look at properties and educate yourself. I'm sure the agent will be happy to cooperate with you to provide this preliminary

16 Units - Polk Avenue - Memphis, Tennessee
Recent Purchase Price:        $91,000
Closing Date: March, 1999
Unit Mix        16-2 bedroom 1 bath
Scheduled Monthly Rents     $2,575

information. Let the market speak to you first by going out and looking at the properties. After you've done that, you'll be able to get more specific in your discussion about properties that you *genuinely* have an interest in because you've seen them and the neighborhoods where they are located.

Once you've educated yourself and selected a few properties that you have an interest in, then your questions will be more specific, such as:

**1. How long has the property been on the market?**

**2. How long has the present owner owned this property?**

**3. Why is the Seller selling the property?**

**4. When were the rents last raised?**

**5. Does the owner provide any appliances?**

**6. Who pays the utilities?**

**7. Who manages the property now?**

**8. How old is the roof?**

**9. Is this owner willing to provide any financing?**

**10. Have there been any other offers on the property?**

**11. Is it possible to see 1 or 2 units to get an idea of the floor plan of the units?**

These questions will allow you to really zero in on the opportunity to see what the real story on the property is. Every property has a story (or history) and the more of it you can learn, the better off you are. The following are reasons for asking the above questions to assist in your decision making.

**Q #1.** If the answer to this question is "4 months or more," it suggests that the property could be overpriced. Don't assume that because it's been on the market a long time that it's necessarily overpriced, or that there is a problem with the property. I can't tell you the number of times I've had a property sit on the market for what I thought was a long time and someone came along after 5 or 6 months and fell in love with the property and did extremely well with it. It turned out to be just what they were looking for. That is why you don't want to jump to any conclusions; just listen and absorb the information. **Q#2.** If the owner has owned the property a short period of time, say less than two to three years, this would suggest that the owner is experiencing some difficulty or frustration with the property and wants out, which suggests that there is real motivation to sell. It could also be possible that the owner bought the property at a bargain price and is trying to make a quick profit. If the owner has owned the property a long time, say 15 years or more, you may have a golden opportunity on your hands. The rent probably has not been keeping up with the market. If the numbers work for you at the present rents, you may be able to get in and substantially raise the rents. Again, listen to the story of the property. If the owner has owned the property a short time and is experiencing some difficulty or frustration, or is looking for a quick profit, it still could be a good deal for you. Be patient and listen.

**Q#3.** This is a very important question and you should never buy a property without asking it. Sometimes, you might ask it more than once and get different responses. However, if you sense that the present owner has had some difficulty with the property, *be sure* you understand what that difficulty is and be sure it is something you feel you can comfortably overcome. Don't be a victim of the "bigger fool syndrome." This is where a Buyer buys something and discovers he was a fool to buy it and he turns around and tries to find a bigger fool than himself to take it off his hands. The fact of the matter is that some apartment buildings can have problems, major problems. These problems can be structural, such as faulty plumbing or electrical problems or management problems, or a building full of tenants who are destroying the property and not paying the rent. *Beware of these properties*, and believe me, if these kinds of problems exist, you will be able to identify them.

**Q#4.** You want the answer to this question to determine if there is room to raise rents in a short period of time. Remember, you are managing efficiently when you're getting the most income from the property. The value of the property increases as the income increases over time.

**Q#5.** Appliances are provided in many markets by custom. The thing to remember is that appliances require maintenance and ultimately, replacement. Therefore, when you do your official walk-through inspection, be sure to note the condition of the appliances.

**Q#6.** Utilities can vary in the amount and depending on the construction, who is responsible for paying the bill. As a general rule, it is better to have a situation where the tenant is responsible for paying the utilities since, as a landlord, you normally cannot control how much those utilities are used. In our market in Memphis, with duplexes, tenants pay all of the utilities. In buildings of three units or more, the owner pays for water and exterior lighting. There are some buildings here that still use steam or radiator heat where the owner pays the heating bill. There are also those instances where some owner will bill the tenants directly for the utilities by prorating the bill among the units in the building. This arrangement is usually spelled out in the tenant's lease so they understand on the front end that they are paying their share of utilities.

14 Units - Orchid Court - Upland, California
Recent Purchase Price:     $607,300
Closing Date: July, 1999
Unit Mix:12-2 -bedroom 1 bath
2-3 bedroom 2 bath
Scheduled Monthly Rental Income  $8,250

Q#7. This lets you know how carefully the property is being watched and monitored. As a general rule, an individual owner will usually keep a closer eye on what's going on with the property than a property management company will, especially on a building of eight units or less. Management companies typically manage a lot of buildings, and as a general rule, don't have the manpower to have someone constantly on site at a smaller building except when there is a problem. This question may not reveal a major issue one way or the other; it's just good to know.

Duplex – Dorothy - Memphis, Tennessee
Recent Purchase Price:      $88,500
Closing Date: April, 1999
Unit Mix: 1-2 bedroom 1.5 bath
1-3 bedroom 1.5 bath
Scheduled Monthly Rents      $1,250

Q#8. One of the major replacements of any building cost-wise is the roof, and they all have to replaced sooner or later. It is nice to know if you will need to replace one soon.

Q#9. This question is an indication of flexibility on the part of the owner. There is usually less cost involved if the owner is able to provide the financing. This is particularly true if the down payment and other terms are reasonable.

Q#10. This is nice to know and it <u>might</u> indicate if you have a flexible Seller or not. If there have been no offers, yours could be the first, and the Seller might be excited to get one to the point that he's more flexible than he otherwise would have been if the reverse was true and there were multiple offers on the property.

**Q#11.** It's a good thing if you can get in to take a look at a few units before you make your final decision. Sometimes the size of the apartment and the floor plan can give you an idea as to how easy it will be to rent.

8 Units - Sunkist Street - Ontario, California
Recent Purchase Price:        $240,000
Closing Date: March, 1999
Unit Mix               7-2 bedroom 1 bath
                       1-3 bedroom 1 bath
Scheduled Monthly Rental Income  $4,175

The classified ads are a good source of information about duplexes and apartments. Most major newspapers will have an "Investment Property for Sale" or an "Income Property for Sale" section. Many realtors and individual property owners will advertise the properties they have available in this section. You can call these individuals and get the information you need to educate yourself about the opportunities in your market.

Finally, the networking approach could be another possibility for finding opportunities in the marketplace. This would involve letting the people with whom you come in contact know that you are an investor in the market looking for opportunities. These people could include contractors, such as roofers, plumbers, electricians, local lenders, and neighbors. Word will start to get around and you will begin to hear about opportunities in your area.

10 Units – Lauderdale - Memphis, Tennessee
Recent Purchase Price:     $98,000
Closing Date: September, 1999
Unit Mix       10-2 bedroom 1 bath
Scheduled Monthly Rents     $1,915

14 Units - Palmetto Avenue - Ontario, California
Recent Purchase Price:          $470,000
Closing Date: June, 1999
Unit Mix:  4-studio
3-1 bedroom 1 bath
7-2 bedroom 1.75 bath
Scheduled Monthly Rental Income  $5,700

# CHAPTER 6 - LOOKING AT THE NUMBERS

In most markets around the country where multi-family properties are sold, information is provided to prospective Buyers and other realtors on a form often referred to as a "setup sheet" or "property profile." This form gives pertinent information about the property being offered for sale. The following information is usually provided with this form.

**Unit Mix:** This is the number of bedrooms and baths in each unit and their monthly income.

**Monthly Rental Income:** This is the amount of scheduled rent when all the units are occupied.

**Taxes:** These are the city and county taxes for the year.

**Insurance:** This is the insurance premium for the year. Most owners carry a fire and a liability policy.

**Utilities:** This is the monthly utility expense. Most landlords pay the cost of water and outside lighting on buildings of four units or more.

**Lot size:** The dimensions of the lot go here. If the dimensions are not available, the total square footage is provided.

**Year Built:** This is the year the building was constructed.

**Appliances:** These are the appliances the landlord provides. This can vary from a stove, refrigerator and/or dishwasher to no appliances.

**Heating:** The type of heating system provided can be central heating, floor furnace or a boiler system.

**Cooling:** The type of cooling system is usually a central heating or widow units. In some markets, no air conditioning is provided.

**Roof Type:** The type of roofing system is usually pitched with shingles, wood or a flat roof.

**Square Footage:** The total square footage of the building is provided here.

4 Units – Azalea - Memphis, Tennessee
Recent Purchase Price:        $59,000
Closing Date: August, 1999
Unit Mix        4-2 bedroom 1 bath
Scheduled Monthly Rent      $935

50 Units - San Antonio Avenue - Ontario, California
Recent Purchase Price:      $1,785,323
Closing Date: May, 1999
Unit Mix        42-1 bedroom 1 bath
8-2 bedroom 1 bath

22 Units - Pauline Avenue – Memphis, Tennessee
Recent Purchase Price:      $350,000
Closing Date: February, 2000
Unit Mix        16-2 bedroom 1 bath
6-2 bedroom 1.5 bath
Scheduled Monthly Rents #7,390.00

Duplex – Haynes - Memphis, Tennessee
Recent Purchase Price:     $55,000
Closing Date: September, 1999
Unit Mix      2-1 bedroom 1 bath
Scheduled Monthly Rents     $675

From the information provided on the profile or setup sheet, you should be able to put together an operating statement. Let's look at one and draw some conclusions from it.

**NOW SELLING**

| **Unit Mix**<br>Sixteen 1-BR, 1-BA @<br>$200 per month |
| :---: |

**Monthly Rental
Income**
$3,200

**Schedule Annual
Rents**
$38,400

**Taxes**
$2,100

**Insurance**
$1,608 Annually

**Utilities**
$960 Annually

**Lot Size**
100 x 200

**Year Built**
1960

**Appliances**
Stoves & Refrigerators

**Heating**
Wall Furnances

**Cooling**
Window Units

**Roof Type**
Pitched Shingle Roof

**Square Footage**
9,600 sq. ft.

## 16 Units    $192,000

## 123 Main Street

Comments:
A nice Garden style apartment building is available near downtown. The units have mostly long term stable residents. The income in $3,200 per month. Please drive by before scheduling appointments.

Directions:
Take Riverside Drive (N) to Beale Street. Take Beale Street (East) to Main Street. Take Main Street (South) to 123 Main Street.

OASIS Apartment Properties, LLC
Jeffrey and Juliette Moore, Realtors
6373 North Quail Hollow Road, Suite 202
Phone: (901) 842-2230
Fax: (901) 842-1113

REALTOR®

## OPERATING STATEMENT
### 123 Main Street
### Memphis, Tennessee

|  |  | Monthly | Annually |
|---|---|---|---|
| 1. | Gross Scheduled Income (16 units @ $200/month) | $3,200 | $38,400 |
| 2. | Less (vacancy factor) 5% | 160 | 1,920 |
| 3. | Gross Operating Income | $3,040 | $36,480 |
| 4. | Expenses: |  |  |
|  | Property Taxes | $ 175 | $ 2,100 |
|  | Insurance | 134 | 1,608 |
|  | Utilities | 80 | 960 |
|  | Manager | 150 | 1,800 |
|  | a. Lawn care | 50 | 600 |
|  | b. Maintenance/Repairs | 165 | 1980 |
|  | c. Supplies | 50 | 600 |
|  | d. Legal | 17 | 204 |
|  | e. Accounting | 25 | 300 |
| 4. | Total Expenses | 846 | 10,152 |
| 5. | Net Income | $2,194 | $26,328 |
| 6. | Less Debt Service (Mortgage Loan Payments $153,600 at 9% for 20 years, payable @ $1,382/month | 1,382 | 16,584 |
| 7. | Cash Flow (spendable income) | $ 812 | $ 9,744 |

6 Units - Bedford Lane - Newport Beach, California
Recent Purchase Price:      $802,500
Closing Date: May, 1999
Unit Mix        4-1 bedroom 1 bath
2-2 bedroom 1 bath
Scheduled Monthly Rents     $5,350

1. "Gross Scheduled Income" is the total income from the property when the property is fully occupied. In our example, that figure is $3,200 per month, or $38,400 per year.

2. "Vacancy factor" takes into account the fact that the property does have vacant units from time to time due to tenants moving and the owner renting to new tenants. We are using a factor of 5% or $1,920 a year. When we deduct the Vacancy Factor from the Scheduled Income, we arrive at a figure referred to as "Gross Operating Income."

3. This number is the number that more accurately reflects the income that the building generated for the year.

4. Next, we deduct from Gross Operating Income the "Expenses" for the year. This is where we take into ac-

count fixed and variable expenses of operating the property. We discussed fixed expenses earlier, such as property taxes, insurance, utilities, and lawn care. However, "Variable Expenses" in our example are as follows:

a. Management - This owner has a part-time Resident Manager whom he pays $150 per month to assist in managing the property.

b. Maintenance - This owner paid $1,980 for maintenance and repairs to the property through the year.

c. Supplies - The owner paid $600 for the year for items such as light bulbs, window screens, and smoke detectors.

d. Legal - The owner hired an attorney to start an eviction procedure against a tenant that he decided he no longer wanted in the building.

14 Units
Lauderdale
Memphis, Tennessee
Recent Purchase Price:          $99,500
Closing Date: February, 1999
Unit Mix          14-2 bedroom 1 bath
Scheduled Monthly Rents     $2,605

e. Accounting - The owner's accountant charged him $300 for the preparation of the schedule relating to this property on his tax return.

These expenses are not always reflected, and will vary from property to property due to the fact that some owners handle all or a portion of these expenses themselves. Therefore, the owners would not pay the additional money to have these things done. Once we account for these items, we arrive at Total Expenses for the building in the amount of $10,152. We deduct the Total Expenses from the Gross Operating Income to arrive at the "Net Operating Income." This number is a very important number! This is the amount we have available to make any mortgage payments on the property if there is a mortgage. If the property is free and clear, this is the amount that the owner has to put in the bank as profit for the month to spend as the owner chooses. In our example, there is a mortgage. The mortgage payment is $1,382 per month. This is based on a loan amount of $153,600 at 9% interest amortized over 20 years. After deducting the mortgage payment, the property still shows a spendable income of $812 or $9,744 per year.

In an earlier section, I illustrated the 4-steps to the formula to increasing your income. Step 3 was to use the income from the property to maintain the property and pay off the mortgage. If the owner in our example took half of the cash flow and placed it in a reserve account for maintenance, and the other half to pay down the mortgage, the mortgage could be paid off in 12 years at a payment of $1,748 per month instead of $1,382. If you took that approach after 12 years, this property alone could pay you a minimum of $2,194 per month for as long as you continue to own it. You would need to have $526,560 cash in the bank paying 5% interest to achieve that same amount of income. This is the awesome income power that multi-family properties can provide with a strategic plan! Finally, the owner of this property could raise the income by $320 per month by raising the rents by $20 per unit.

6 Units - Miramar Drive - Newport Beach, California
Recent Purchase Price:        $700,000
Closing Date: May, 1999
Unit Mix        5-1 bedroom 1 bath
                1-2 bedroom 1 bath
Scheduled Monthly Rents     $5,313

Once you have completed this analysis of the property, you should be ready to make some decisions about whether to proceed with the purchase of the property. The property clearly has cash flow sufficient to cover the normal operating expenses of the property, as

69

well as to provide income necessary to pay the proposed mortgage off in 12 years or less and provide a reserve for future repairs and maintenance.

If you are comfortable with the appearance of the property, the neighborhood where it is located, and the history of the property that you have been able to obtain, it is time to take steps towards owning the property yourself.

14 Units - Danny Thomas - Memphis, Tennessee
Recent Purchase Price:        $82,000
Closing Date: October, 1998
Unit Mix        6-1 bedroom 1 bath
                8-2 bedroom 1 bath
Scheduled Monthly Rents     $2,500

# CHAPTER 7 - LET'S MAKE A DEAL (IT TAKES COURAGE!)

I think it's important for an investor, particularly a beginning investor, to understand the fact that as you start to get comfortable with the ownership and acquisition of income properties, you will occasionally run across what may be considered to be a super deal. By super deal, I mean the property is priced at what's considered to be a bargain, given its location and income. However, the mistake that I see investors make all too often is trying to buy a property only if it is considered a super deal. I've got news for you. If you take that approach, you will miss out on many opportunities that turn out to be great deals for the Buyer. Many deals do not seem to be great deals on the front end.

I always suggest that you do your analysis of the property based on the asking price of the property. If the numbers make sense and the investment feels right based on that, and you are able to get a lower price or better terms on the deal than you originally planned for, then that makes it that much sweeter.

This is the *Action Stage* of this process. This is where one has to have the *courage* to believe in themselves and act. I have come across many individuals in my years of doing this business who look at property after property–analyzing, scrutinizing, trying to look at the deal at every angle, worrying about whether they missed something, worrying about how much profit the Seller is going to make, asking the same questions over and over again–and never taking action. They simply don't have the courage to stop dreaming and to make this thing real for themselves. It takes courage! I can't over-emphasize this fact.

16 Units - Maple Avenue - Costa Mesa, California
Recent Purchase Price:     $1,975,000
Closing Date: May, 1999
Unit Mix        All-2 bedroom 2.5 bath
Scheduled Monthly Rents     $17,306

I can show you everything you need to look at and understand about this process, but please understand that there is *risk*. It is an investment and there are things that can go wrong. There can be repair items that you didn't prepare for, or a tenant who refuses to pay or can't pay, but doesn't want to move without being forced out. Things happen and believe me, all of us who are landlords or income property owners occasionally have a bad experience. However, we understand that a bad experience should not shake our confidence in the power of income property to provide us with substantial income and wealth. Instead, we learn from that experience and move on.

You have to make offers to make good deals in this type or any type of real estate. Rarely does a property sell for full price or on exactly the price and terms that the owner indicated that he would take. Everything can be negotiable. Let me also repeat that sometimes a good deal, possibly a great deal, may not appear to be so great on the front end. The price the Seller is asking may seem too high. The rents may appear to be too low. The expenses could appear to be too high, etc.

Let's talk about an approach that I would encourage you to consider at this stage of the game. In most cases, individuals who decide to sell their income properties are not hurting to sell their buildings or desperate to sell them. Trust me on this. After being involved in the negotiations and closing of over $100 million dollars in apartment transactions in my career, I know that this is often the case. Therefore, let's assume the Seller is not desperate for cash or hurting to sell. We need to approach each deal with the idea that we've done our homework and the numbers work, so we want to do what we need to do to *own the property*. That should be our focus. The only way we can get the benefits that ownership of the property provides is to *own the property*. Anything short of that keeps us on the sidelines as an observer and not in the game as a player. We need to be absolutely clear about that.

Given that mindset, let's approach the acquisition of a building, the one we previously analyzed, and here

12 Units - Walker Avenue - Memphis, Tennessee
Recent Purchase Price:      $65,000
Closing Date: May, 1999
Unit Mix        12-1 bedroom 1 bath
Scheduled Monthly Rents     $1,740

is the situation: The owner of this building is asking $192,000 cash for this 16-unit apartment building. Let's make the owner an offer and start the process toward owning this property.

Let's follow the items in Exhibit A, which is a typical Purchase Contract:

**Earnest Money Deposit:** The earnest money deposit is $3,000. The earnest money is held by the broker in a trust account until the closing and then brought to the closing. It is brought to the closing by the broker and paid to the closing agent or closing attorney on behalf of the Purchaser.

**Personal Property:** This clause is used to spell out any appliances to be transferred to the Purchaser at closing.

**Purchase Price:** The price is spelled out in words and numbers. We'll offer a price of One Hundred Seventy-two Thousand Eight Hundred dollars (90% of the asking price.) There is no magic formula here. I am suggesting an offer of 10% less than the asking price because in the example we are serious and want to own the property. The deal makes sense, even at the asking price, so we are simply trying to sweeten the deal for ourselves. Remember, the objective is to own the property, not simply to make offers for the sake of making offers. My experience has been that the chances of the deal getting done are substantially increased when the Buyer's initial offer is at least 90% of the asking price.

14 Units - Rochester Street - Costa Mesa, California
Recent Purchase Price:       $2,020,000
Closing Date: June, 1999
Unit Mix       14-3 bedroom 2.5 bath
Scheduled Monthly Rents     $16,833

# OASIS Apartment Properties, LLC
## CONTRACT FOR SALE AND PURCHASE OF REAL ESTATE

PARTIES. This Contract is made and entered into by and between (please print full name):

_Joe Seller_ ("Seller") and

_Ronald Purchaser_ ("Purchaser")

As used herein, where applicable, "Purchaser" and "Seller" include the plural; masculine includes the feminine and neuter gender. **EARNEST MONEY DEPOSIT:** Received of Purchaser the sum of _Three thousand_ Dollars (\$_3,000.00_) as Earnest Money in the form of (check, money order, etc.) _check_ to secure Purchaser's performance of this Contract and to be applied as part payment of the purchase price. Purchaser and Seller agree that the Listing Agency/Broker will hold the Earnest Money in trust, subject to the terms of this Contract.

**REAL PROPERTY:** Subject to the terms and conditions of this Contract, Seller agrees to sell and Purchaser agrees to purchase the following described real property (including the personal property) located in the County of _Shelby_, City of _Memphis_, State of _Tennessee_, known as: (Please print street address or legal description.) _123 Main Street_ all permanent improvements thereon are hereinafter collectively referred to as "Property."

**PERSONAL PROPERTY:** The purchase price includes any and all appliances being provided to the residents of the properties that are owned by the Seller.

**PURCHASE PRICE:** The total purchase price for Property shall be _One Hundred Seventy-two Thousand Eight Hundred_ Dollars (\$_172,800.00_), payable in all cash at closing, of which Earnest Money is a part.

**FINANCING:** This Contract is contingent upon Purchaser obtaining a written loan commitment for approximately _80%_ within _30_ calendar days at terms and conditions acceptable to Purchaser. Purchaser agrees to make loan application for this loan within ten (10) calendar days of this contract and to use diligence to obtain this loan.

**TERMITE INSPECTION:** Seller agrees to furnish a letter or report from a reliable state licensed and bonded termite control operation, stating that the residence is free from active termite or wood destroying insects. Seller shall have such treated and/or repaired if termites and/or structural insecurities and/or water or moisture problems are found. The cost of any necessary treatment and/or repairs because of such wood destroying insects or water or moisture problems, will be paid by Seller up to a maximum of _2,000_. Said letter or report shall be issued during the period preceding the closing date. Seller will not be held responsible after closing.

**PROPERTY CONDITIONS, INSPECTION AND ACCEPTANCE OF PROPERTY:** Purchaser agrees to accept the property including without limitation all improvements, plumbing, heating, electrical, air-conditioning, built-in appliances, with no warranties or representations, either expressed or implied, having been made by Seller or Seller's agent or representative, **subject to Purchaser's inspection and approval.**

**CONVEYANCE AND TITLE:** Seller hereby agrees to sell and convey Property or cause it to be conveyed, by good and sufficient warranty deed, unto Purchaser or unto such persons as Purchaser may designate; Purchaser, however, shall not be released from any of Purchaser's agreements and undertakings as set forth herein, unless otherwise stated herein; and Purchaser hereby agrees to purchase Property from Seller, subject to and upon the terms and conditions set forth in this Contract. Title is to be conveyed subject to all restrictions, easements of record, zoning ordinances and all other laws of any governmental authority, covenants of record, articles of association or incorporation, by-laws master deed, any rules and regulations, and amendments thereof.

Seller agrees to furnish Purchaser for examination only either title search or adequate abstracts of title, taxes, judgments and liens as soon as same can be prepared covering Property, or, at Seller's option, an owner's title insurance policy for the amount of above purchase price insuring a good and marketable title which shall constitute and be accepted by Purchaser as conclusive evidence of a good and marketable title. Adequate abstracts of title, taxes, judgments, and liens shall be as required by a title insurance company authorized to do business in the State of Tennessee. Purchaser's closing attorney shall choose Title Company.

**BROKER'S FEE:** Seller agrees to pay OASIS Apartment Properties, LLC a ten percent (10%) real estate commission at closing.

**CLOSING, ATTORNEYS AND TITLE COMPANY:** The closing shall be on or before _October 30, 2000_. Unless otherwise stated herein, closing agent/attorney will be _purchaser & seller's choice_

**OCCUPANCY:** Occupancy will be given subject to any existing lease agreements at closing.

**SALES EXPENSES TO BE PAID IN CASH AT OR PRIOR TO CLOSING:**

A. **Seller's Expenses:** Prepayment penalties on any existing loans to be paid at closing, plus cost of releasing such loans and recording releases; Seller's closing fee, document preparation fee and/or attorney fees; preparation of deed; notary fee on deed; title search or abstract. Seller authorizes closing agent or attorney to order title search or abstract from the title company set forth above. **A Transaction Fee of \$295 shall be paid to OASIS at closing, to offset cost of coordinating inspections with tenants. Said fee is hereby waived if property is vacant and to remain vacant during term of contract.**

**CASUALTY LOSS:** The improvements on Property are to be delivered in as good condition as they are as of the date of this Contract, ordinary wear and tear excepted. In the event, prior to closing, of total or partial destruction by fire, or other casualty, with damage to the improvements located on Property in excess of 10% of the above purchase price, then Purchaser may cancel this Contract and all of the Earnest Money shall be refunded to him; otherwise, in the event Purchaser does not elect to cancel this Contract, or in the event such damage is equal to or less than 10% of the above purchase price, Seller shall have the obligation to repair such damaged improvements by the closing date as stated above. In the event of destruction by fire, or otherwise, Seller's liability shall in no event be more than the appraised value of the improvements so destroyed.

**DEFECTIVE TITLE:** If the title is not good and cannot be made good within a reasonable time after written notice has been given that the title is defective, specifically pointing out the defects, then the above Earnest Money shall be returned to Purchaser and the brokerage as specified in the listing agreement plus all costs of collection shall be paid by Seller.

**BREACH OF CONTRACT BY PURCHASER:** If this agreement is breached by Purchaser or if Purchaser fails for any reason to complete his purchase of this Property in accordance with the terms set forth herein, Seller shall have the right to elect to declare this Contract null and void, and upon such election, the Earnest Money shall be retained by and divided equally between Seller and real estate brokers as liquidated damages and brokerage respectively, but in no event shall the real estate brokers' share exceed the broker's commission as specified in the listing agreement. The right given Seller to make the above election shall not be Seller's exclusive remedy, as he shall have the right to elect to affirm this Contract and enforce its specific performance or recover full damages for its breach. Seller's retention of such Earnest Money shall not be evidence of an election to declare this Contract null and void, as Seller shall have the right to retain his portion of Earnest Money to be credited against damages actually sustained. In addition to any other remedies available against Purchaser by any party to the Contract because of Purchaser's failure to close for any reasons other than those permitted by this Contract, Purchaser shall be obligated to pay the real estate commission due Broker herein had Purchaser not breached this contract.

**BREACH OF CONTRACT BY SELLER** If this agreement is breached by Seller or if Seller fails for any reason to complete the sale of this Property in accordance with the terms set forth herein, Seller shall pay damages in an amount equal to the real estate commission due had Seller not breached this contract, plus attorney fees and costs. In the event of default by Seller the Earnest Money shall be returned to Purchaser and Purchaser shall have the right to affirm this Contract and enforce its specific performance.

**COSTS TO ENFORCE CONTRACT:** Should any party to this contract bring an action against any other party to this Contract to enforce any claim hereunder, the prevailing party or parties shall be entitled to recover all costs of said action and reasonable attorney fees. The term "prevailing party" as used in this Paragraph shall be defined as the party or parties in whose favor a court shall rule, or against whom no relief is granted, which becomes final and non-appealable.

**ESCROW:** The Earnest Money is deposited in escrow with the Listing Agency/Broker ("Escrow Agent") with the understanding that Escrow Agent (a) is not a party to this Contract and does not assume or have any liability for performance or non-performance of Seller or Purchaser, (b) has the right to require from Seller and Purchaser a written release of liability of the Escrow Agent which authorizes the disbursement of the Earnest Money, (c) is not liable for interest or other charge on the Earnest Money, and (d) may choose to place the Earnest Money with a Court of competent jurisdiction in the event of any dispute. If the Escrow Agent shall file any interpleader, Escrow Agent shall be entitled to recover its attorney fees and expenses from the Earnest Money deposit. If Seller or Purchaser unreasonably fails to deliver promptly the document described in (b) above, then such parties shall be liable as stated above. At closing, the Earnest Money shall be applied to any cash down payment required, then to Purchaser's closing costs, and any excess refunded to Purchaser. Written evidence from the bank showing clearance of any monies must be presented before any money will be released prior to 14 days from deposit.

**ENTIRE AGREEMENT:** This Contract contains the entire agreement of the parties relating to the subject matter hereof and cannot be changed except by their written consent. The following addendum(s) are a part of the contract: (list and attach or, if none, print NONE ): See Addendum A _____

_____

**NOTICES:** All notices shall be in writing and effective upon delivery to the party at the addresses shown below.

**CONSULT YOUR ATTORNEY:** None of the brokers or agents, if any, can give you legal or tax advice. This is intended to be a legally binding Contract. **READ IT CAREFULLY.** Federal law may impose certain duties when Seller and/or Purchaser is a foreign party, or Seller receives a certain amount of U.S. currency in connection with a real estate closing. IF YOU DO NOT UNDERSTAND THE EFFECT OF ANY PART OF THIS CONTRACT, CONSULT YOUR ATTORNEY OR TAX CONSULTANT BEFORE YOU SIGN THIS CONTRACT

**EXECUTED** by Seller and Purchaser on the date(s) shown below their respective signatures. NOTICE: The date upon which this contract is fully executed and finally accepted by the Seller and Purchaser and the date the Earnest Money is available for deposit is the date shown below as the contract effective date.

**CONTRACT EFFECTIVE DATE** _____, _____

**PURCHASER:**                          **SELLER:**

_____          _____

_____          _____

_____          _____
Purchaser's Address/Telephone Number          Seller's Address/Telephone Number

**Financing:** This is the financing contingency in the contract. If the Purchaser is unable to obtain financing, the Purchaser has the option to cancel this agreement and have the earnest money returned.

**Termite Inspection:** The Seller agrees to provide a termite clearance here and agrees to complete repairs necessary to provide a clearance up to $2,000.

**Property Conditions, Inspection, and Acceptance of Property:** The Purchaser agrees to accept the property "as is" subject to the Purchaser's inspection.

**Conveyance and Title:** Seller agrees to provide clear title to the property with this clause.

**Broker's Fee:** The commission to be paid to the real estate broker is spelled out here.

**Closing, Attorneys, and Title Company:** The closing date and closing attorneys are indicated here.

**Occupancy:** This clause is used to alert the Purchaser to the fact that any existing leases will be transferred at closing.

**Seller's Expenses:** This clause spells out the expenses that are normally the responsibility of the Seller at closing in my area.

**Purchaser's Expenses:** This clause spells out the expenses that are normally the responsibility of the Purchaser at closing in my area.

**Proration:** This clause addresses the items that are to be prorated at closing.

**Casualty Loss:** This clause addresses any major damage or destruction to the property that could occur after the contract is signed and prior to closing.

**Defective Title:** In the event Seller cannot deliver clear title, the Purchase shall have the option to cancel and have the earnest money returned.

**Breach of Contract by Purchaser:** This clause addresses the possibilities in the event all contingencies in the contract are satisfied and the Purchaser does not close.

**Breach of Contract by Seller:** This clause addresses the possibilities in the event all contingencies in the contract are satisfied and the Seller does not close.

**Costs to Enforce Contract:** In the event of legal action as a result of this agreement, the losing party shall have the obligation to pay the attorney fees of the winning party.

**Escrow:** This clause talks about how the earnest money is to be handled.

**Entire Agreement:** This clause is where any addenda that will be a part of the contract are identified.

Page 3 of the Purchase Contract is the *Apartment Addendum*. Addendum A is herein made a part of the agreement. This addendum should be made a part of any standard residential purchase contract in that it addresses items that are relevant to the purchase of apartment buildings and duplexes that may not be covered in a typical residential contract.

1. These items are to be provided to the Buyer for review and approval within so many days after the contract has been signed.

2.a. This report is usually required on up to 4 units where the owner has occupied one of the units.

2.b. This clause protects the Buyer from having the Seller rent to tenants they would not normally rent to just to get a few extra dollars prior to closing, or modifying an agreement in a way that would not be acceptable to the Buyer. Most Sellers don't engage in any of these practices, if for no other reason than the fact that the possibility always exists that the deal may not close.

2.c. This gives the Buyer the opportunity to inspect the property again prior to closing.

# Addendum A

This is an Addendum to that certain contract For Sale and Purchase of Real Estate dated ___July 1, 1900___ in which ___Ronald Purchaser___ is referred to as Purchaser and ___Joe Seller___ is referred to as Seller regarding the property known as ___123 Main Street___, hereinafter referred to as the Subject Property.

1. LEASE/SERVICE AGREEMENTS AND INCOME/EXPENSE STATEMENTS: Within __7__ calendar days of written agreement herein, Seller shall make available to Purchaser for Inspection and review the following items checked below:

☒ All current leases
☒ All contracts entered into by Seller affecting the property
☒ A rental statement including tenant names, rental rates, last rent increase, and any remaining deposits

☒ An operating statement for last __24__ months
☐ Other: _____
☐ Other: _____
☐ Other: _____

Seller represents that the records provided above are true and accurate to the best of Seller's knowledge. Disapproval of the above to be in writing to Broker within __3__ days of receipt, otherwise this contingency shall be deemed removed.

2. Other agreements check below are INCORPORATED HEREIN:

☐ A. SELLER'S DISCLOSURE REPORT: (Up to 4 units only) Seller agrees to provide Purchaser with a Property Disclosure Report within _____ calendar days from written acceptance herein, buyer and Seller agree that Purchaser shall have three (3) days after delivery of Property Disclosure Statement to Purchaser to terminate this agreement by delivery of written notice of termination to Seller or Seller's agent.

☒ B. CHANGES PRIOR TO CLOSING: Prior to closing of this transaction, Seller agrees not to: (1) rent or lease any vacant unit on other than a month to month basis, (2) alter, modify or extend any existing rental/lease agreement or (3) enter into, alter, modify or extend any service contract, (4) without first having obtained Purchaser's approval.

☒ C. FINAL WALK THROUGH INSPECTION: Seller shall provide Purchaser with access to interior of all units within five (5) calendar days prior to closing to insure that (1) all appliances, plumbing, heating and electrical systems and mechanical fixtures functioning properly, (2) any corrective work agreed to by Seller has been accomplished, (3) property and improvements are in the same general condition as when contract was signed by Purchaser and Seller, Buyer's deposit of remaining down payment at closing shall constitute Buyer's approval of final walkthrough.

☐ D. SALE OF PURCHASER'S PROPERTY: Purchaser's obligations hereunder are conditioned upon the close of Buyer's real property located at _____ within the time specified herein for closing. Buyer's above referenced real property is ☐ currently listed for sale or exchange, ☐ currently under contract for sale or exchange and scheduled to close on or before (date) _____.

☐ E. PURCHASER'S EXCHANGE CONTINGENCY: Purchaser and Seller agree that the close of this transaction shall be contingent on Purchaser effecting a tax deferred exchange qualifying under Section 1031 of the Internal Revenue Code. Seller agrees to execute such documents or instruments as may be necessary or appropriate and reasonable for purchaser to evidence such exchange. Purchaser shall have the right to substitute and/or assign Purchaser's position as Purchaser of the property to a Third Party who shall acquire the property in its name, and subsequently transfer the property in whole or in part to Purchaser for purpose of exchange. Purchaser's down-leg property is ☐ currently listed for sale or exchange, ☐ currently under contract for sale of exchange and scheduled to close on or before (date) _____, ☐ has already closed.

☐ F. SELLER'S EXCHANGE OPTION: Seller shall have the right and option to convert this transaction into a tax-deferred exchange qualifying under Section 1031 of the Internal Revenue Code, provided, however, that Seller shall not prevent or delay the closing as provided herein and also provided that Purchaser shall be at no additional cost, expense or liability.

☒ G. SELLER'S EXCHANGE CONTINGENCY: Seller and Purchaser hereby agree that the closing of this transaction shall be contingent on Seller effecting a tax-deferred exchange under Section 1031 of the Internal Revenue Code. Purchaser agrees that if by date of _____ Seller has not delivered to Purchaser a copy of a Purchase contract entered into by Seller providing for the acquisition of Seller's exchange (up-leg) property on or before the closing date as provided herein.

☒ H. SECURITY DEPOSITS/KEYS/LEASES: All security deposits, a minimum of one (1) set of keys for each unit, and any remaining original lease agreements shall be transferred to Purchaser at closing.

☒ I. VACANT UNITS: Any vacant units are to be rent ready (painted and cleaned) at closing.

☒ J. PAST DUE RENTS: All past due rents shall be collected by Seller prior to time of closing and all collections made by Purchaser after closing shall accrue to the sole benefit of Purchaser.

☒ K. WALK THROUGH INSPECTION: This transaction is contingent on Buyer conducting a walkthrough INSPECTION of all units within __7__ days of acceptance of this Contract. Buyer will submit any disapproval of the subject property in writing to Broker within __3__ days of walkthrough inspection; otherwise, the walkthrough inspection shall be deemed approved.

☒ L. EXPIRATION DATE: This offer to purchase shall expire if not accepted, or a counter proposal executed, no later than _____ July 6, 2000 ___.

☐ M. ADDITIONAL CONTRACT TERMS AND CONDITIONS: _____
_____

2.d. If the Buyer is selling a property to acquire the property in this contract, this clause would be used.

2.e. If the Buyer is selling a property and completing an exchange transaction, this clause would be used.

2.f. If the Seller wants to do an exchange with the proceeds from the sale, this clause would be checked.

2.g. If the Seller *will only sell the property if an exchange can be completed,* this clause would be checked.

2.h. These items should always be transferred to the Buyer at closing.

2.i. I usually use this clause prior to closing.

2.j. This clause is for the purpose of making it clear that all rents collected by the Purchaser are for the Purchaser and not for the Seller.

2.k This is the Buyer's initial formal walk-through inspection and should allow the Buyer to inspect every unit.

2.l. We need to reach agreement by this date.

2.m Any additional terms not previously covered that need to apply to this transaction are added in this section of the contract.

Finally, our objective as individuals creating wealth and substantial incomes for ourselves is to *own multi-family properties.* For this to happen, we must make *reasonable offers* that the owners of those properties will agree to and sign. That's the only way we get to play the game. Otherwise, we're just spectators. If you're making reasonable offers in the market, you will be closing transactions, taking ownership of income properties, and increasing your income and wealth in the process.

Duplex - Woodhollow Avenue - Memphis, Tennessee
Recent Purchase Price:       $74,900
Closing Date: May, 1999
Unit Mix       2-3 bedroom 2 bath
Scheduled Monthly Rent         $1,000

# CHAPTER 8 - FINANCING OPPORTU-
# NITIES - "THERE'S MONEY EVERY-
# WHERE!"

There has not been a better time than the last couple of years to obtain financing for your income property opportunities. We will talk here about some distinctions in obtaining financing that you should be aware of without getting too complicated.

First of all, there is a major difference in obtaining financing for duplexes, triplexes, and four-plexes, vs. buildings containing five units or more. Two to four-unit properties are treated almost the same as single family homes, and are classified as residential properties. The rates that one pays for the financing of these properties is almost identical to the rate one would pay for a single family home, whether owner-occupied or not. Therefore, in most markets around the country, there are numerous lenders available to make these loans. The qualifying process for those buildings is very similar to that of single families in that the lender looks at a certain ratio of the Buyer/Borrower's income to the outstanding debts. The credit rating of the Buyer according to a credit report from the various credit reporting agencies is also evaluated.

With 2- to 4-unit properties, the Buyer does gain a slight advantage in qualifying, due to the fact that 75% of the rental income of the property is used to help qualify the Buyer. Therefore, where a Buyer may only qualify for $100,000 as a Buyer of a single family home, that same Buyer would qualify for a higher sales price if they are buying a duplex, triplex, or four-plex.

10 Units - Hamilton Street - Costa Mesa, California
Recent Purchase Price:        $902,500
Closing Date: April, 1999

The major types of financing available on 2-4 unit properties are FHA and conventional. With FHA, a Buyer usually can pay *less than 10% down* to acquire the property. *FHA does require the Buyer to occupy one of the units in the property.* This occupancy must take place within a certain time after the closing. In many cases, all of the units in the property will be occupied at closing. Therefore, after closing, the Buyer will need to give a 30-day notice to vacate to the tenant occupying the unit the Buyer will eventually move into. VA loans fall under the same guidelines as FHA loans as far as underwriting goes. VA loans, however, allow a veteran Buyer to be able to acquire a property with no down payment as long as he meets the income and credit criteria. VA loans are also available on up to 4-unit properties.

The maximum loan amounts for FHA and VA loans as of this writing are as follows:

Duplexes up to $144,450
Triplexes up to $175,500
Four-plexes up to $202,500

In the more expensive markets around the country, loan amounts may be slightly higher, based on the cost of housing in that particular market.

Conventional financing differs from FHA in a few distinct ways that are important to investors. Most importantly, conventional loans are available that do not require the Buyer/Borrower to occupy one of the units. The property can be an investment only. Maximum loan amounts will typically go up to 80% of the purchase price, with the Buyer paying 20% cash down. However, in many markets, there are lenders that will go up to 90% of the purchase price. This represents a golden opportunity for investors in these markets because by obtaining financing with 10% down an investor has an opportunity to use that extra cash to acquire more properties. These loans also affect the Buyer's income, and the income generated by the property determines the Buyer's ability to qualify. The maximum loan amounts for conventional loans on 2 to 4 unit properties can be slightly higher than FHA and VA loans. The maximum amounts are as follows:

Duplexes up to $307,100
Triplexes up to $371,700
Four plexes up to $461,350

Duplex – Philwood - Memphis, Tennessee
Recent Purchase Price:       $82,500
Closing Date: March, 1999
Unit Mix       2-2 bedroom 1 bath
Scheduled Monthly Rents    $850

Conventional loans usually make up the majority of financing available on apartment buildings of 5 units or more. This source of financing can sometimes be a challenge to obtain because the majority of these loans are classified as *commercial loans* and as such, are evaluated differently from 2 to 4 unit "residential" loans. However, in many markets, local banks are the primary sources for these loans.

There are other loan programs available through FHA and/or HUD that are geared for large apartment properties and that are available for the rehabilitation of those properties. I have not gotten involved with those programs because they tend to be much more complicated and restrictive. However, they do exist, and if you call or write HUD, I'm sure they would send you information on those.

Qualifying to obtain financing on any of the previously mentioned programs, such as FHA, VA, or conventional, is going to require that you, as the Buyer, meet certain guidelines. The lender that will be providing the financing will cover these issues with you. However, be prepared to provide the following information to the lender:

a. Verification of your current income in the form of current pay stubs.

b. Last two years of tax returns.

c. Current credit report (most lenders will obtain this on their own at your cost.)

9 Units - Delaware Street - Huntington Beach, California
Recent Purchase Price:       $942,000
Closing Date: March, 1999
Unit Mix:   1-1 bedroom 1 bath
7-2 bedroom 1.5 bath
1-3 bedroom 2 bath

d. Verification of the funds needed to close (bank statements.)

e. Rent statement on the property you're acquiring (this statement provides the amount of rent paid by the tenants for each apartment.)

f. Copies of leases of the existing tenants.

g. An operating statement on the property for the past year or two (a statement of the past year's rental income and expenses.)

Once the lender has all of this information, he can fully evaluate the borrower and the property to decide if he will make the loan. Until the lender has all of this information, it is usually difficult to make a decision.

Once your loan has been approved, based on these items, the Lender will usually issue an approval of the loan, contingent upon the property being appraised for an amount at least equal to the purchase price. It is at this time that the lender will have you, the Borrower, pay for the cost of the appraisal. It is then ordered and scheduled. Once it is completed and submitted to the lender and acceptable, your lender will then notify you that they are ready to close and a closing date is set as soon as possible.

If it happens that the appraised value comes in at less than the purchase price, the options available to you as the Buyer are to:

1. Go back to the Seller and attempt to renegotiate the price to equal the appraised value. (The Seller is usually under no obligation to do this, and it usually depends on the Seller's motivation.)

2. Pay the difference between the amount the lender is willing to loan based on the appraisal and the purchase price (depends on how good a buy the property is for you), or:

3. Cancel the transaction, since you are unable to get the amount of financing you intended, and have your earnest money returned to you.

Finally, there is a lot of money available in the market today to finance the acquisition of apartment buildings. As an investor, you should be prepared to pay a minimum of 10% of the purchase price as a down payment, along with paying closing costs that can run from 2 to 5% of your purchase price, depending on the type of loan it happens to be.

Let me also mention an additional financing source that we haven't talked about up until now, and that is the Seller. It is becoming less common for the owner to provide financing. However, if you are able to find a deal where the owner is in a position to provide financing, this can be your best source. This is primarily due to the fact that there are none of the loan costs involved that are present when a loan is obtained from an outside lender. The transactions that are financed by the owner can close much faster. In some instances, we have closed them in less than a week. The critical aspect of obtaining owner financing is making sure that the terms (interest rate and amortization period) are terms that the building can support. An owner is usually going to require a minimum down payment of 10% to 20%.

Please remember that regardless of what your amortization period is for the loan, whether it's the owner or one of the other sources we have talked about, in most cases, there is no prepayment penalty. This means that if you choose to, you can make payments above your normal mortgage payment. This will enable you to pay off the loan sooner and own the property free and clear ahead of schedule.

4 Units - Forelle Drive - Huntington Beach, California
Recent Purchase Price:        $448,000
Closing Date: May, 1999
Unit Mix        3-2 bedroom 2 bath
                1-3 bedroom 2 bath
Scheduled Monthly Rents    $3,525

# CHAPTER 9 - DUPLEXES - EVERYBODY SHOULD KNOW

Some of the best kept secrets, it seems, in the arena of real estate ownership and investment are the benefits available to the individuals who acquire a duplex as owner-occupants. In other words, the individual buys the duplex and instead of renting both sides, the Buyer moves in on one side and then rents the remaining unit to a tenant.

For many, this strategy continues to be the launching pad for getting started in real estate investment. That's due to the fact that there are many advantages to the individual who adopts this approach to getting started in real estate ownership and investment. Some of the more important advantages are: 1. minimum down payment requirements, 2. favorable interest rate, 3. tax benefits, 4. ease of management, and 5. income.

**Minimum Down Payment** - The Buyer who intends to buy a duplex to live in can finance the purchase using the FHA loan. FHA requires the least amount of cash down from the borrower, usually less than 10%.

**Favorable Interest Rate** - The Buyer who acquires a duplex as an owner-occupant receives a better interest rate than a Buyer who would be acquiring that same duplex, but with the intention of simply renting out both units. The owner-occupant Buyer would be entitled to the same interest rate as someone buying a single-family residence under the FHA program even though that owner-occupant Buyer has every intention of renting out the additional unit.

Duplex - Oak Park - Memphis, Tennessee
Recent Purchase Price:     $81,000
Closing Date: July, 1999
Unit Mix      2-3 bedroom 2 bath
Scheduled Monthly Rents     $990

**Tax Benefits** - The tax benefits for an owner-occupant of
a duplex Buyer are the same as they are for the owner of
a single-family residence. That is, the owner is entitled to
deduct mortgage interest, and in some cases, deduct
property taxes as well. However, in addition to those
deductions, the duplex owner may also deduct expenses
for certain repairs, insurance, and depreciation. Consult
your accountant or tax preparer as to the amount of
those deductions, but they are available in addition to
the deductions normally available to a homeowner.

**Ease of Management** - The duplex in this case is easier
to manage for the owner simply due to the fact that the
tenant is next door. Most of the time-consuming aspects
of management, such as meeting prospective tenants

92

when there's a vacancy, meeting maintenance professionals when repairs need to be made, or collecting the rent from a tenant are minimized when the owner lives next door.

**Income** - Undoubtedly the most important advantage available to the duplex owner is the additional rental income that in most cases, is going to pay most of the mortgage payment. In fact, in many cases, when one takes into account the tax benefits of ownership, along with the income from the rented unit, it usually equates to the duplex paying for itself and the owner's housing cost being totally eliminated. For example, let's assume a Buyer acquires a duplex for $85,000 and moves into one side. The mortgage payment, including taxes and insurance, equal $725 per month. The Buyer rents the additional unit for $625 per month. Tax benefits to the new owner equate to $2,400 per year or $200 per month. See the illustration in Exhibit 1. One can see that this owner's mortgage payment is covered by the rental income and

4 Units - Demion Lane - Huntington Beach, California
Recent Purchase Price:     $454,000
Closing Date: May, 1999
Unit Mix      3-2 bedroom 2 bath
              1-3 bedroom 2 bath
Scheduled Monthly Rents     $3,525

tax benefits and yet the owner is occupying a nice home. What a deal! In addition to this obvious benefit, the Buyer of an owner-occupied duplex does not need to make the same amount of income to qualify as the Buyer of a single family home trying to qualify for that same mortgage amount. That's because the lender, in qualifying the duplex Buyer, will take into account the income received from the additional unit and factor usually 75% of that rent into the Buyer's income.

Given these benefits, one can easily conclude that buying a duplex is worth serious consideration as a *first step* in real estate ownership.

**Exhibit 1:**

|  | Monthly |
|---|---|
| **Rental Income** | **$625.00** |
| **Tax Benefits** | **$200.00** |
| **Total** | **$825.00** |
| **Less: Mortgage Payments** | **$725.00** |
| **Net Income to Duplex Owner** | **$100.00** |

*The owner has a net income (after taxes) of $100 per month while reducing the housing cost to zero because the rent and tax benefits more than cover the mortgage payment!

# CHAPTER 10 - CREATIVE FINANCING

People sometimes are confused about the term "creative financing." It is often felt or assumed that "owner financing" is "creative financing." Others believe that creative financing takes place when the Buyer acquires a property with "no money down."

I believe that both of the previous examples are examples of creative financing. In fact, I would conclude that any time a property is financed in a manner that is outside of the normal 20% down payment and 80% new loan, it qualifies for consideration as a "creative financing" technique.

I would like to share some of the more common methods that have been used over the years to "creatively finance" the acquisition of apartment buildings.

**100% Financing - Line of Credit and Owner:**
With this technique, a property has been located where an owner has indicated that he would sell the property and provide 80% of the financing. The Buyer does not have the other 20% in cash necessary to complete the deal. However, the Buyer has owned his personal residence a long time and has a lot of equity in the property. The Buyer approaches his bank about obtaining a line of credit secured by the equity in his home. The bank approves the line of credit and the Buyer uses it for the down payment, the closing costs, and an operating reserve.

*Points to remember:* Owner financing was provided in this deal, but only up to 80% of the sales price. Usually, the Seller who is providing the financing will want to see the Buyer have some investment in the property, even if it is borrowed.

The Buyer has to have a decent credit rating to be able to qualify to obtain the credit line.

Be sure that the property can support the additional payment created by the line of credit.

## 100% Financing - New Loan and Owner:

With this technique, a property has been located where an owner may be willing to provide financing, but only up to 20% of the purchase price. The Buyer approaches a bank or other lender about providing the remaining 80% of the sales price. The lender approves the Buyer and property and makes an 80% first mortgage loan on the property. The Seller carries a second mortgage loan on the property.

*Points to remember:*

The Buyer will need to have a strong credit rating and financial statement to qualify for this financing.

The Seller can sometimes be hesitant about this type of financing unless there is a *strong need* for cash. This is due to the fact that the Buyer has no cash invested in the property. The Seller is also carrying a 2nd mortgage behind a 1st mortgage of 80% of the purchase price. If the Buyer defaults (is unable to pay) on the 1st mortgage, the Seller will need to step in and make payments on the 1st mortgage to protect the Seller's financial interest in the property. Otherwise, the bank could foreclose and take the property wiping out the Seller's 20% 2nd mortgage.

## Split-Down Payment - Owner Financing:

With this technique, a property has been located where an owner is willing to provide financing up to 80%, for example. The Buyer does not have the remaining 20% at the time the deal is being negotiated. The Buyer offers to pay 10% down at closing, and the remaining 10% over a two-year period with equal semi-annual payments.

5 Units - Roosevelt Lane - Huntington Beach, California
Recent Purchase Price:        $735,000
Closing Date: April 1999

*Points to remember:*
The Buyer should be sure of the source of funds that will retire the remaining 10% balance. Ideally, cash flow from the property will provide this.
The Seller will probably want to approve of the Buyer's credit rating and financial statement with this technique.
**Exchange and Sellout:**
        With this technique, a property (Property A) has been located where the owner has a large equity and is interested either in acquiring a larger property, or simply getting the cash out of the property as soon as possible. The Buyer is interested in the property, however, the Buyer needs to sell a smaller property to complete the transaction (Property B).

An offer is made to buy Property A contingent on the owner of Property A buying Property B so that the smaller property owner can have the cash required to complete the purchase of Property A. The owner of Property A was not in the market for a smaller property, however, since the purchase of the smaller property provided the cash necessary to sell Property A, the owner ends up with the majority of the cash from Property A, and a small equity in Property B, which is immediately put on the market to be sold.

Duplex - Baltic Avenue - Memphis, Tennessee
Recent Purchase Price:        $60,000
Closing Date: September, 1999
Unit Mix        2-2 bedroom 1 bath
Scheduled Monthly Rents        $650

*Points to remember:*
This technique makes sense for both parties, especially if the prices that both owners are asking is reasonable.

Either owner could take the initiative and make the offer and neither has to sit back and wait on a Buyer to come along.

With this technique, the Buyer of Property A is not using cash, but rather his equity in Property B to acquire the property.

**Purchase and Re-Fi Out:**

With this technique, a property has been located that can be acquired for a price substantially below appraised value. The Buyer has the cash and resources to buy the property, but does not want to tie up the cash required to do the deal for an extended period of time–two years or more. The Buyer finds a lender that would be willing to lend up to 80% of the appraised value of the property. The Buyer closes on the property, and after one year, refinances the property and pulls the cash back out.

*Points to remember:*

The Buyer may want to consider having the property appraised prior to closing to ensure that the value will be sufficient to allow for the refinance. The Buyer will need to be able to qualify for the refinance.

The techniques of acquiring property with creative financing mentioned above are the more common approaches that I have seen successfully used in the acquisition of apartment buildings. I'm sure there are other techniques that have been used to acquire investment property. The key to any financing scenario would be making sure that the property can support the financing that is being used.

4 Units - Almond Avenue - Orange, California
Recent Purchase Price:      $385,000
Closing Date: April, 1999
Unit Mix: 1-1 bedroom 1 bath
2-2 bedroom 2 bath
1-3 bedroom 2 bath
Scheduled Monthly Rents    $3,150

# CHAPTER 11 - TAX DEFERRED EX-CHANGES

There are many owners of investment property who sell their investment properties and take the proceeds from that sale and buy other investment property, paying capital gains tax on any profit they made from the sale. This is not always considered the best use of one's hard-earned capital. This is because the IRS allows us to structure our transactions so that when we sell an investment property and we buy a property of equal or greater value with the proceeds, there is no capital gains tax due. This process is covered under Section 1031 of the United States Tax Code and is one of the aspects of the tax code of which all investors should be aware.

As a practical matter, it is not necessary for us to be able to recite the code verbatim, we simply need to find closing attorneys, escrow officers, brokers, or any of the professionals who will be involved in our transactions who understand how this process works.

As a real estate investor, you need to know a few basic criteria to be able to complete your transactions; your professionals can take care of the details. Here are some rules to keep in mind:

1. The investor has 45 days from the day the transaction closes on the property being sold to identify a replacement property. Identification is simply stating in writing the addresses of the properties being considered. There is a limit on the number of properties that can be designated in writing. There is no limit on the number of properties one can consider however. This just means

4 Units – Vineyard - Ontario, California

that one needs to only designate in writing the properties that one intends to pursue seriously with the intention of entering into a contract.

2. The investor has *180 days* from the day the transaction closes on the property being sold to close on the replacement property. There is no flexibility in that date.

3. The property or properties replacing the property being sold must be equal to or greater in value (sales price) than the property being sold. For· example, if I sold a property for $300,000, I must replace it with a property or properties that total at least $300,000 in price.

4. The replacement property can be any type of property that is to be held for investment. It does not have to be the same type of property. For example, land can be replaced (or exchanged) for an apartment building, office building, industrial building, shopping center, or other land, or vice versa. Any type of investment property can be exchanged for any other type, including single family homes used as rentals. This is a very important point because many investors get confused by the term, "like

kind," which is used in the tax code. However, that term simply refers to investment property for investment property vs. investment property for a personal residence.

5. The investor should always indicate on the contract with the property being sold, as well as the contract for the replacement property, that it is the investor's intention to do a tax-deferred exchange.

4 Units - Randle Avenue - Memphis, Tennessee
Recent Purchase Price:       $70,000
Closing Date: September, 1998
Unit Mix       4-1 bedroom 1 bath
Scheduled Monthly Rents      $925

6. The investor shall have his closing agent (either escrow company or closing attorney) locate an intermediary to hold the investor's proceeds from the sale if the replacement property is not ready to close at the same time the property the investor is selling closes. The in-

vestor cannot receive the proceeds from the sale at closing. They must be held by the intermediary until the replacement property is ready to close.

The 1031 tax-deferred exchange is not a complicated process once you understand the steps involved. Usually the biggest challenge is the timing involved in the sale of the property the investor is going out of. I usually like to have the investor actively looking for a replacement property while we are attempting to find a Buyer for the property the investor is selling. In some cases, if the Seller's motivation and situation made it possible, we have completed deals where the Seller of the replacement property accepted the investor's property that was to be sold. We would continue to try to find a Buyer for the investor's property. However, we could go ahead and close on the replacement property as soon as possible.

4 Units - Florida Street - Huntington Beach, California
Unit Mix      4-2 bedroom 1 bath
*The first apartment building I ever owned and managed.

# CHAPTER 12 - MAY WE CLOSE NOW?

The final step in acquiring ownership of the apartment building is the actual closing of the transaction. For your closing attorney or escrow company to be able to close your transaction there are several items that will need to be in place. The following is a list of those items and the person who typically is responsible for being sure that they are handled by closing time:

| Closing Item | Person Usually Responsible |
|---|---|
| a. Copy of Purchase Contract | Broker |
| b. Buyer's Earnest Money | Broker or Closing Attorney |
| c. Title Policy | Closing Attorney or Escrow Officer |
| d. Insurance | Buyer and Broker |
| e. Loan Documents | Lender |
| f. Tenant's Security Deposits, Keys and leases | Owner |
| g. Survey | Lender, Closing Attorney |
| h. Termite Inspection Report | Seller and Broker |
| i. Rent statement | Owner and Broker |

These items are all brought to the closing and are all a part of the process that takes place. The Buyer and Seller should always bring a picture form of identification to the closing, as many of the documents that will be signed will need to be notarized. The funds that the Buyer will need to close should be in certified funds (cashier's check usually). Most closings are very simple and take less than an hour to complete, especially if there are no unusual circumstances, and the parties in-

105

volved in the closing have had sufficient time to prepare everything. A couple of points you should take note of regarding the closing of a transaction are as follows:

1. All parties who are on the loan and taking title to the property, such as husband and wife, or partners, will need to sign the HUD-I closing statement along with other closing documents provided by the lender and closing attorney.

2. The termite inspection is usually done prior to the closing, and after the final loan approval has been obtained.

3. Most Buyers obtain their own insurance. The policy usually will cover fire and liability only if the property is for rental purposes only.

4. Rents are usually prorated as of the day of closing and the Seller usually transfers all security deposits to the Buyer. Those deposits, however, belong to the tenants and should be placed in a separate account.

5. Letters are usually sent to all of the tenants from the Seller the day after closing informing the tenants that the property has sold.

6. After closing, the utility companies should be notified to transfer the utilities that are paid by the Seller to the new Buyer. In many cities a deposit may be required by the utility company to transfer the utilities to the new owner.

72 Units - Poplar Avenue - Memphis, Tennessee
Recent Purchase Price:        $953,000
Closing Date: February, 1999
Unit Mix: 4-1 bedroom 1 bath
68-2 bedroom 1 bath
Scheduled Monthly Rents    $19,500

# CHAPTER 13 - MANAGING FOR MAXIMUM INCOME

You've closed on the apartment building and you are now ready to take on the task of managing it so that it can inflate your income as planned. A lot of folks seem to complicate this issue of property management as though it requires a degree in rocket science. I like to keep it simple. The success of your management plan depends on four basic factors. They are: 1) tenant screening, 2) property maintenance, response time to repairs, 3) collections, and 4) marketing vacant units.

**Tenant screening** is important because the tenants in your building are the customers you are choosing to do business with. You provide a service and you need to have customers who will be pleasant to work with and who can afford to pay and are willing to pay for your service. Always be sure to have them complete an application that will require the following information: a) their current employer, b) current address, and c) Social Security number. Have them sign an authorization to run a credit check. We also run background checks to determine if they have been involved in any criminal activity. You should check their income and find out how long they've been on their present job. After all, their job will be their main source of income, and thus your main source of payment for the rent. In most cases, it helps to know that there is stable employment. It is also good to know where the applicant previously lived and under what circumstances they left. It is one thing to leave because you need a larger apartment, or a nicer one, or a better location, etc. However, it is another story when the tenant is being evicted for non-payment of rent. Find out what you can about that tenant.

If they can't or won't provide you with this basic information, it's a sign that they might become a problem tenant. Most management companies suggest that a prospective tenant's income should be at least 3-4 times the amount of the rent as a minimum. This could be a reasonable benchmark when you start to get $300/month or more in rents. One thing to remember when screening your tenants is that getting them out if they turn out to be a problem can be much more difficult than letting them in. Be careful. A bad tenant or problem tenant can cause your good tenants to move, and can destroy your apartments in the process if you're not careful.

**Property maintenance** is important to attracting and keeping good tenant prospects. When you maintain the property so that it has a nice appearance, the existing tenants will take pride in it as well. Proper, timely property maintenance is critical. Replacing and painting rotted boards and keeping the grounds neat are things that help to make the property more attractive. When you have a vacancy, it's important that you have the unit rent ready (cleaned and painted) before you attempt to show it to a new prospective resident. It is very important that the first impression that your apartment gives is a good one. It follows logically that if you attempt to show units that are not well kept, you are sending a message to prospective residents that it's okay for them to live any kind of way in the unit. It's worth it sometimes to take the necessary time to make sure the unit is presentable, even if it seems as though you have a prospect who is ready to move in right away and can't wait to see the apartment. It's important to have your team of people who will get the unit ready prepared to work on it as soon as it becomes vacant. You should assemble a team of reliable people to do the following types of work: Plumbing, painting, electrical, carpentry, heating and air conditioning repair, general cleaning, carpet cleaning, and carpet installation. A good roofer is also important to have. Of course, these professionals are all helpful if you own a home that needs repairs from time to time, and not just for your income property. Occasionally, you will find individuals we call "handymen" who have the skill to do a variety of things. It's good to know them because they can save you time due to the range of skills they have. When a unit becomes vacant, a handyman and/or carpenter will probably need to get in the unit first to get their jobs done. Once any repairs are completed, the unit is ready to be painted. Most experienced painters can do some of the carpentry and prep work needed to be done before the painting is to begin. Once the painting and cleaning have been done, the unit can be shown unless the carpet shows poorly. The carpet should be cleaned, if possible, or replaced.

I'm sure it's quite obvious that as an owner of an apartment building or duplex, there are some financial requirements outside of the cost of acquiring the property. Unfortunately, many new owners are unprepared to deal with the additional maintenance and repair issues that are a part of ownership's responsibility and they become frustrated with this aspect of the process. This is quite common and understandable. I've found that the new owners who have done well with the transition to becoming an owner are those who have already thought through the maintenance aspect of the business. They have predetermined *before closing the deal* how they are going to deal with a vacancy and who they will use for the different phases of getting the unit rent-ready. They have an idea what those jobs will cost and have determined how they will deal with those costs.

It's a good thing to set up a maintenance reserve account that will be used to deal with maintenance and repairs. That account can be funded from the cash flow from the property even though it is initially set up with funds from your personal resources. Simply keep track and reimburse yourself as soon as possible so that the building carries itself financially. However, be prepared

20 Units - Poplar Avenue - Memphis
Recent Purchase Price:        $210,000
Closing Date: March, 1999
Unit Mix:        20-1 bedroom 1 bath
Scheduled Monthly Rents    $3,500

as much as possible to deal with unexpected costs that could come up in excess of your reserve account. The focus should be on the fact that the property, when properly managed and maintained, will pay for itself and pay you substantially for the rest of the time that you own it.

Another fundamental aspect of successful management is the time that an owner or manager takes to respond to requests for repairs from the residents. It is important to respond quickly with reliable and responsible repairmen. Many landlords fall down in this area unnecessarily. Remember that these residents are your customers. If they have to wait long periods of time whenever they have a repair problem, or experience the frustration of having to fix the same thing over and over again because it wasn't done right the first time, eventually they will take their business elsewhere. That's why it's important to have that team of repair specialists in place as soon as possible prior to closing. Tenants who are happy with your level of service will stay with you and pay on time. However, the opposite is also true. Those who are unhappy will move often or not pay on time.

**Rent collections** are a critical component to efficient management of your property. It's important that you and your residents have an understanding that you expect your rent to be paid timely if they expect to continue to live there. As soon as the transaction closes, the tenants should be sent a letter from the previous owner or management company indicating that the property has been sold. It should indicate who the new owner is, and that the rent for the next month should be paid to the new owner. You, as the new owner, should write a letter to the tenants letting them know how the rent is to be paid. (A sample letter is provided in Exhibit B.)

## EXHIBIT B

### Introduction Letter to Tenants

November 15, 1999

Mr. Joe Jones
23 Main Street
Apartment #1
Memphis, TN

Dear Mr. Jones:

This letter is to inform you that the property you now occupy has been sold. The new owner is <u>OASIS Apartment Properties</u>.

Rent for the month of December should be paid to OASIS and mailed as follows:

> OASIS Apartment Properties
> 6373 North Quail Hollow, Suite #101
> Memphis, TN 38120

If you have any repair requests or questions, please call our office at 842-0000.

Thank you for your cooperation. We look forward to working with you.

Sincerely,


OASIS Apartment Properties

Some landlords provide tenants with self-addressed envelopes and have them mail the rents to them if the properties do not have an on-site manager. If the rents are not received by the 6th of the month, there is a late charge. If I have not received the rent by the 15th of the month, a letter is issued indicating that the tenant is in violation of the Lease Agreement and reminding them to pay immediately, vacate the property, or risk being evicted. If I don't receive the rent, plus the late charge, by the 20th, the eviction process is started, and I don't stop it once it is started. Experience has taught me that once a tenant doesn't pay in a given month, it's time to start the process to get that tenant out and find a new tenant.

I'm sure that policy in regard to rent collection varies a great deal from owner to owner. Many owners like to go out and collect the rent themselves rather than have the tenants mail it. Others have it dropped by their office. My philosophy has always been that if the tenant is going to pay the rent, they are going to pay it, and, therefore, I use the most convenient means for me to receive it. Many landlords let a tenant get a couple of months to several months behind before they will start an eviction, and will stop the process as soon as the tenant pays. There are no hard and fast rules. You have to decide what works best for you. It's a good idea to talk with other investors and see what they do. Also, it's important to ask around and find a person, usually an attorney, who is experienced and has a good reputation for handling evictions.

Usually, when you discover you have a bad tenant on your hands, it's important to move quickly and decisively to get that tenant out of your property.

Be sure that all of your tenants have signed a lease that you keep in your files. The length of the lease period can vary from one year to six months, or can be a month-to-month agreement. I prefer a one-year lease agreement. At the end of the initial year, this agreement becomes a month-to-month, which allows either party to terminate the agreement with a 30-day notice to the other. Notice must be given prior to the 1st of the month. Some landlords use month-to-month agreements. Most areas of the country vary as far as to what is commonly used. It depends upon the amount of flexibility you feel you need to have in dealing with your tenants.

**Marketing vacant units** is a critical component to your cash flow and the overall success of your operation. It is important to get vacant units rent-ready as soon as possible. Once they are ready to show, there are two basic ways most landlords use to get them re-rented. The first is to place a "For Rent" sign in the front yard with a phone number for prospective tenants to call. If you keep the property looking nice on the outside (building exterior and grounds), you should get calls from this approach that will lead you to your next tenant. The second approach, in addition to the "For Rent" sign, is to advertise in the classified advertising section of the newspaper. The proper way to word your ad is simply to be descriptive, but brief. I always include the rental amount in the ad. In addition to these techniques, we offer a referral to our existing tenants if they refer a tenant to us who will decide to rent. The main point to remember is to be active and aggressive when marketing your vacant unit.

Managing your apartment building will be much more efficient and prosperous if you: a) screen your residents, b) prepare in advance for the maintenance of your property, respond quickly to your tenant's repair request, c) have clear-cut collection policies, and d) market your vacant units aggressively.

# CHAPTER 14 - THE MISSING INGREDIENT

It has been a very exciting time to be in the investment real estate business for the last few years. Markets around the country are seeing record-breaking activity in sales. The U.S. economy is in the best shape it has been in over the last 20 years. In fact, after nearly two decades of record budget deficits, there is a budget surplus. What all of this means to individuals like you and me is that prosperity is available like never before in our lifetime and it's up to us to reach out and grab our share.

Apartment buildings offer one of the best real estate investments of our time. In fact, the popularity of apartment building ownership and the demand for this type of investment is at an all time high. It's available to such a wide variety of people because of the versatility in size and price range that it offers. It's not limited to wealthy investors or large investment groups. Individuals with $5,000 cash can participate, as well as those individuals or groups with $1 million or more to work with. That's a huge spectrum of people and possibilities. The properties come in all sizes all over the United States. You need to start to research the opportunities available in your market and begin to acquire properties in your backyard.

If you have ever seriously considered the possibility of acquiring an apartment building or duplex for income, now is the time to do it. I believe in taking the long-term approach to acquiring the property and managing it efficiently so that the income covers its operating costs and pays off the mortgage over a 10- to 15-year period. At that point, you have an asset that can pay you for the rest of your life, or if you have a major emergency and need a lump sum of cash, it can be borrowed against to provide that. However, the main reason I love apartment buildings is the income! The income generated by apartment buildings is what makes them the most sought-after commercial real estate investment in the country.

There is no equal commercial real estate investment that can provide the benefits to as broad a range of individuals. One building can provide the income equal to a lifetime of savings. For example, let's say you own free and clear an apartment building consisting of six units that generates a net income to you, after expenses, of $1,500 per month. Let's say that building cost you $30,000 down to acquire it. To reach that same amount of income from a bank or financial institution at 5% interest, you would need to have saved $360,000. That's right! $360,000 at 5% interest generates the income of a $30,000 investment in an apartment building that cost $150,000 and generates $1,500 per month net income. Assuming the building cost $150,000 when it was acquired, there is a good chance that with very little inflation, the income has increased over time. The building, more than likely, is easily worth over $200,000. That means you not only have a great return as far as monthly income, but you have an asset worth over $200,000 that you acquired for $30,000. That's over 600% return on your investment over 15 years.

However, we can talk all day about how great an investment in apartment buildings can be. There is one ingredient that is missing and standing between you and a substantial income in apartment buildings. That ingredient is something this book, any other book, or lecture on this subject, cannot provide. That ingredient is simply the courage to make it happen for yourself. Thousands of books on this subject are bought every year and statistics would indicate that less than 5% of the people who acquire this knowledge ever act on it.

Will you be one of the 95% who merely acquire the knowledge and just become well informed? Or will you be one of the 5% who acquire the knowledge, add the courage to make it happen, and go on to build a comfortable income for yourself from the application of this information? It's up to you now. My job is done.

I'd like to think that you have the courage. In fact, I know you have the courage! Release it! I wish you prosperity beyond your wildest dreams!

May God Bless!
Jeffrey B. Moore

# INDEX

# A

Acquisition strategy 35, 36, 39, 40
Action 71
Addendum 79
Advertising 115
Appliances 26, 52
Application 108
Appraised Value 99
Attorney 67

# B

Background check 108
Bigger fool syndrome 53
Breach of Contract 79
Broker's fee 78
Building styles 47
Business 39

# C

Capital 101
Capital gain 101
Cash flow 41
Casualty loss 78
Churches 21
Classified ads 49,57
Clients 36
Closing attorney 75, 76
Closing date 75
Commercial loan 86
Commercial real estate 16, 17, 118
Conventional financing 81, 84
Corporate strategy 30
Creative financing 95
Credit 84, 95

# D

Defective title 78
Depreciation 92
Down payment 47

# Duplex

Duplex 18, 22, 35, 83-85, 91-94, 110, 117

# E

Earnest money 74
Economic opportunity 49
Electrical problems 54
Equity 92, 95, 96
Escrow 79, 103
Eviction procedure 67, 114
Exchange transaction 78
Expenses 66, 67

# F

Faulty plumbing 54
FHA 84-87,91
Financial freedom 39
Financial Statement 97
Financing 24, 52, 78
Floor Plan 57
Four plex 24, 26, 80, 82
Free & clear 41, 42, 43

# G

Gross operating income 65
Gross scheduled income 65, 67

# H

Handyman 110
HUD 83

# I

Income property for sale 57
Industrial buildings 21
Insurance 93, 105, 106
Investment 44

# L

Land 21
Landlord 54, 112, 114

Lawn maintenance 62
Lease 88, 105, 114
Lenders 51
Like kind 102, 103
Line of credit 95
Loan to value 22
Location 46
Los Angeles Rams 17
Lump sum 28, 118

## M

Maintenance 39, 67, 107
Maintenance reserve 111
Money market 33
Month to month agreement
    112
Mortgage 42, 89, 91
Mortgage payment strategy
    42
Mutual fund 33

## N

Net operating income 68
Networking 49
NFL 17

## O

Occupancy 23, 74
Office buildings 21
On-site manager 114
Owner financing 95
Owner-occupant 91

## P

Parcel number 60
Painting 110
Personal property 74
Portfolio 46
Prepay penalty 43, 89
Principal payment 43
Professional football 16
Profit 53, 101
Property profile 60

Proration 78
Purchase price 47, 74

## Q

Quit claim 106

## R

Real estate and urban devel-
    opment 16
Reasonable offers 81
Rehabilitation 86
Rent collection 112
Rent statement 105
Repairs 67
Replacement property 101,
    102
Resident manager 67
Retail stores 21
Retirement 32
Roof 52, 60

## S

Section 1031 of US Tax Code
    101
Security deposit 105, 106
Seller's expense 78
Setup sheet 60
Shopping centers 18, 21
Single family homes 21
Social Security 30
Square footage 60
Stock market 39
Strategy 36, 41
Survey 105

## T

Tax benefits 92
Tax returns 87
Tenants 40, 66
Tenant screening 108
Termite inspection 78, 105

## U

Unit mix 47
University of Tennessee 16, 17
Upscale properties 47
Utilities 52, 54

## V

Vacancy factor 65

## W

Warehouse 21
Wealth 37, 72
Wide Receiver 17